Simple Spirituality

Finding Your Own Way

James C. Nourse, Ph.D., L.Ac.

ISBN: 143822821X
EAN-13: 9781438228211

Cover: One of 88 shrines at the Lawaʻi International Center, Kauaʻi, Hawaiʻi. The Center exists as a "gathering place for all people to hear what is not said, to see what cannot be seen, to feel what cannot be touched, to know peace...where individuals from all parts of the world can get in touch with the vestiges of their spiritual and cultural roots and traditions." Contact *www.lawaicenter.org*.

Cover photograph by Joshua Atkinson
Cover design by Adam Nisenson.

Dedication

This book is dedicated to Dr. Dan Austin, my ninth grade unified studies teacher. His spiritual presence, and his relentless determination to evoke the best in each student, opened the portal to the labyrinthine path that leads to Truth for all of us blessed enough to be encouraged and challenged by him. By his example we were given the opportunity to see that spirituality is neither a creed nor a set of beliefs, but a quality of Being that invites us to awaken from the slumber of ignorance.

Contents

Content today, yesterday not
Moods as weather patterns
Blaming and the high-maintenance self
Awareness that embraces all mind states
Our genetic blueprint for inner peace

Introduction

Over the years many of my psychotherapy clients have found it helpful to discuss their religious histories and their current spiritual beliefs and practices. There was a time not that long ago when people were hesitant to talk about these matters with their therapists, because there was an idea in circulation that most therapists were agnostics or atheists who felt spirituality was sheer fantasy. This fear was not without foundation, as Freud had advocated that religion was nothing but a sort of mass obsessive-compulsive neurosis. From the other side, even therapists who were sympathetic to spiritual concerns had been trained to strictly separate the spiritual from the psychological and to focus only on the latter. Happily, with the emergence of the field of *transpersonal* psychology, it is now viewed as at least appropriate if not advisable for the psychotherapist to permit open consideration of a person's spiritual life in the consulting room. On the one hand, it has become painfully clear that there exists in our world a phenomenon that could justifiably be called *spiritual abuse*, in which a parent, pastor or other authority figure has used spiritual concepts to justify threatening, dominating or harming another person, or terrorizing them by repeatedly invoking and enforcing the image of a wrathful deity who will consign them to eternal damnation if they fail to observe the proper protocol. That spirituality as contained by religion has so frequently been experienced as a stifling, shame-inducing, life-denying affair is one of the great tragedies of the human condition. Spirituality must be, rather, a gateway to internal freedom, relatedness, creativity and joy, an enterprise that evokes and promotes what is best in us.

The psychotherapist must not avoid a discussion of these matters and their emotional impact on the grounds that they concern the spiritual domain. On the other hand, a person's spiritual beliefs and values have become seen as potentially offering important resources for insight and healing of emotional wounds and surviving dark times in a person's life. Either way, to exclude spirituality from the conversation is to hamper both the diagnostic and therapeutic potency of psychotherapy. Additionally, there are some clients who have for whatever reason abandoned the religion of their youth or for whom spiritual or religious ideas have never carried much significance, who begin to find themselves curious about or attracted to spirituality once again or for the first time. Jung noted that it is not uncommon for a person who has undertaken a journey to investigate and heal psyche to be led to the realm of spirit (and vice versa). Typically these individuals are not looking for a denomination or a church, but are sensing that there is something about their lives and about Life that transcends the obvious. Yet, they feel unsure about how to undertake an exploration of this new awareness and at the same time are wary of anyone who seems to have all the answers. Some have asked me, "Is there a book on spirituality I can read?" This repeated question is what has encouraged me to complete this book.

There is yet a third category of person for whom a book on simple spirituality is made to order. This is the spiritually obese individual who has feasted too long at the smorgasbord of teachers, gurus, metaphysical systems and esoteric practices and has an acute case of spiritual indigestion. They may possess a rich knowledge of spirituality and a resume of powerful transformative experiences, but, as T.S. Eliot has said, "between the idea and the reality falls the shadow." For such a person, spiritual knowledge has not translated well into a program for daily living. What is required in this instance is a return to simplicity, to the stuff of immediate experience, less focused on someone else's program and more openness to the seeds of one's own. To the spiritually ravenous, this may seem like a starvation diet. All I can say is that fasting can be transformational.

Without exception, all these individuals complain of being too busy, and of trying unsuccessfully to simplify their lives. Not just coming from psychotherapy clients, this today is the universal complaint. All would agree that any activity that has meaning for us, or that gives our life meaning, must be allotted a certain amount of time and energy. Whether it's our career, our relationships, our hobbies, or our health, an investment of time and energy is required to maintain and improve them. Spirituality is no exception. It won't take care of itself somehow. Yet most of us have no time or energy for one more activity, no matter how meaningful it might be. The key, then, is to be able to identify those areas of one's life that are already in place which can be used in a different way. If we look at time as a horizontal line that is able to contain a finite number of activities and there is no space on that line in which to squeeze something else, then a way must be found to, as it were, draw a vertical line from some of these activities, that represents not a new activity but the quality of one's awareness in and relationship to an activity. Interestingly, this line may be thought of as ascending or descending, which is often how spirituality is characterized, as reflected in such expressions as "heightened awareness" or "deeper understanding."

This book is about that vertical dimension, written for the person who has no time, but for whom spirituality has arrived on the set and is demanding a part in the series. It is written for the person who wants a jump start, but does not want to be taken on a tour. My hope is that it will offer a framework for creating a core spirituality, a scaffolding upon which a person can begin to build his/her own unique spiritual awareness and orientation, geared to and expressive of his/her own unique gifts, discoveries and potentials.

James C. Nourse, Ph.D., L.Ac.

Chapter 1
On the Road

I was on my way to my office in Brevard, North Carolina, heading as usual down Crab Creek Road, a curvy path winding its way through green hills and pastures and mountain vistas. It was a cool, gray spring morning with a gentle rain falling. I slipped a disc of quiet selections into the CD player and leaned back to spend the next half hour waking up enough to begin a day of seeing clients. I can't say exactly when I became aware of it, but at some point I had found my way into a feeling of utter contentment. The grayness of the morning, the lushness of the earth, the metronome of the windshield wipers, the gentle rhythms of the music and the steady movement through the scenery and I as the observer of it all became woven into one fabric, one substance, one mind. I can't say there was any drama in it at all, no great joy, no profound thoughts, no visions or voices. Just a feeling of utter contentment. Later in the drive I became aware that I was no longer wholly in the experience, but was beginning to *think about* the experience. What came to me is that this is the way I want to be able to feel in all aspects of my life, that this is the essence of a spiritual life, finding that sort of deep contentment and connection in the very everydayness of life. Spiritual experience is so often talked about using terms like enlightenment, salvation, transformation -- they may all be pointing to real possibilities, but they are highly charged words that suggest something huge, ultimate and probably very difficult to attain, requiring special disciplines and procedures and major changes in one's beliefs and habits. In other words, beyond the reach of those of us who have to earn a living, raise kids and pay bills. What I realized in this simple experience was that spirituality is just a different take on the scenery we wind our way through every ordinary day. What if we could cultivate the capacity for experiencing life in this way, rather than just waiting and hoping for it to happen?

Since my college days, I have known that spirituality was to be a central focus of my life. By the time I was in my late teens, church had become a negative experience for me. I have given it a few other tries over the years, but somehow I never got the hang of church. With rare exception, the experiences that I described to myself as spiritual seemed to come in ways and in settings that had nothing to do with conventional religion. I came to realize that for me it was useful to distinguish between spirituality and religion. For many people, the two do blend, but not for me. Over the years I have met many other people for whom this is also true. Especially in my psychotherapy practice, I have counseled scores of individuals who have deep spiritual yearnings which, when acknowledged and developed, have become the essential ingredient in their healing process. Often these people have let their spirituality remain dormant because they mistakenly believed that if they did not attend church or subscribe to a major denomination, they weren't spiritual. Others, who prided themselves in their scientific thinking, felt that spirituality was superstition and therefore delusion. Whether a person's spirituality has become trapped in the prison of religion, in the prison of science, or is simply a latent capacity in need of nurturance and growth, there must be a way of bringing it into everyday life without taxing time and energy accounts that are already in default. But spirituality as a concept is nebulous. What do we mean by this term? How do we take it from being just a concept to becoming a force that is active in our lives? This is something I have struggled with in my own life as well as in my professional practice. I can't even remember how many times I have started, and stopped, meditating. I have taught my clients how to meditate, and have sent them to formal meditation classes and they often sheepishly admit after a few weeks that they haven't meditated in awhile. I know exactly what they are experiencing, because I have gone through the same thing. There are many reasons for it, but for whatever reason, other demands displace spiritual practice. The unfortunate consequence is that most people feel a sense of shame and failure about it, that they are too weak or undisciplined or that their problems or responsibilities are just too big to allow them to have a spiritual life. I know.

My brief experience on the drive to Brevard seemed to instruct me to contemplate how one can begin to open to a spiritual life using the materials at one's immediate disposal. Years ago I attended a workshop given by a Native American medicine man. At one point he was looking for some tobacco, a sacred substance in his tradition, to perform a blessing, and he ended up using a

Winston cigarette that he lit with a Bic lighter. Some of us were surprised at the apparent irreverence of this behavior. He laughed and said, "We Indians always feel amused at you white folks when you rub sticks together to make fire at these gatherings. The Indian way has always been to make use of available materials."

So, most of us have a thousand demands on us every day. We are in a hurry a good bit of the time, there is more to do than we can complete, weeks of miscellaneous mail sit in piles, hundreds of emails in the in box, and the car is 2,000 miles past due for an oil change. In the rare moments when we come up for air we know this is no way to live but there seems to be no way off the treadmill. How do we find spirituality in the midst of this relentless onslaught? How do we make use of available materials without having to add one more thing to our to our to-do list? This is what I want to explore with you.

Chapter 2
What Is Spirituality?

There are many ways spirituality could be defined, and as you work with the concepts presented here. you will be able to come up with a definition that makes sense to you. Allow this definition to change as your spirituality grows. For present purposes I will define spirituality as *a type of consciousness which permits a person's everyday life to have a heightened sense of meaning, fulfillment, vitality and peace and a way of relating to whatever one may experience with greater wisdom and compassion.*

Let's examine each element of this definition.

A type of consciousness: Consciousness is something we take for granted. As you read these words, you are, first of all, awake and not asleep, and you are conscious of what you are reading and you are processing the information you are taking in. If you are in a deep sleep state, as far as we know, you are not conscious of anything. If you are dreaming, you are conscious but in a different way from being awake. At least what you are conscious of, with all the strange twists and turns in dreams, is different. Consciousness can be highly focused, as when you are trying to solve a mathematical problem, or it can be diffuse, as when you are relaxing and taking in a sunset. Consciousness can be seen as that very faculty of our makeup that enables us to have experiences. That faculty that converts the energies of the world around us and within us into experiences.

Meaning: A quality of experience that conveys to one's life a sense of rightness and value. A sense that my being alive is better than my not being alive, that it somehow matters that I am here.

Fulfillment: That I possess, or have the capacity to access, an experience of contentment and satisfaction in my life that is not dependent on whether I get my own way. As opposed to *pleasure*, which comes from the external world gratifying my desires, fulfillment is a state of being arising from within myself, and may be experienced in the presence of either pleasure or pain, getting my own way or not, joy or sadness.

Vitality: The experience of really being alive.   Energy, enthusiasm, commitment, passion, and devotion are words that come to mind in describing vitality. Vitality can be quiet and reflective, or loud and expressive. It is life-force, and is what provides the impetus to grow, to move ahead, learn, expand, relate, love.

Peace: This is a faculty we have that allows us be present to and patient with what is, what is presenting itself to us whether from within or without, without having to act on it, change it, or fix it in any way. It allows us to experience conflict with another person, or between different feelings within ourselves, without getting all riled up. This aspect of spiritual consciousness creates a container that values all standpoints and allows them all a safe and receptive place to exist and express themselves. It enables a state of comfort to come about with *not knowing*, and thereby depressurizes the situation.   Often it is the sense of pressure that leads to violence or to a hasty decision to resolve an inner conflict that ends up causing more problems than the decision was designed to resolve. Beginning in a state of peace, even when confronting war, we are more likely to end in peace.

Wisdom and Compassion: I combine these two faculties because one cannot really exist without the other. It is possible to view wisdom as a faculty of the mind and compassion as a faculty of the heart, but in spiritual consciousness mind and heart must be integrated in order for either to achieve its true value. To be truly wise, wisdom must be compassionate and to be truly compassionate, compassion must be wise. Wisdom is the capacity to see deeply and with clarity into the nature of the world, and to perceive accurately the relationships between the different factors and features of a situation, and to be able to comment or act in a way that is helpful. Wisdom, seeing as it does the interrelationship of all things, sees also the suffering that is so much a part of life, and cannot help but be moved by it and motivated to help alleviate it. In this fashion, it ventures into the territory of compassion. Compassion is the ability to relate to another person or situation or other feature of our experience with love, and with a sense of what will relieve suffering in a way that is best for all concerned. Compassion does not ignore the needs of the giver nor does it necessarily give all. There is a parable about continuing to give a hungry man fish to eat vs. teaching him to fish. Sometimes compassion can come in the form of tough love, of seeing what someone needs in order to get out of the rut they're in, rather than continually gratifying their momentary desires. But tough love is a tough decision, isn't it, as those of you who have lived with an alcoholic or a difficult teenager can attest. To do what's right for someone when they have a different idea about it, to respect your own boundaries while ministering to others, are examples of how compassion requires wisdom to be effective. On the other hand, an astute appraisal of a complex situation delivered as an intellectual analysis can be felt as a stab to the heart, and displays no wisdom whatsoever.

As already suggested, this definition of spirituality, including the definitions of its elements, is not complete, and never can be. Perhaps it can be a starting point for you, a way to begin exploring and developing your own understanding of spirituality. Note that the terms God, or even Higher Power, were not included in this definition. There will be more said about this later. Spirituality is a natural feature of our human experience and evoking it and growing with it enables us to live happier lives, and this ability is granted to anyone who is willing to cultivate it, whether religious devotee or atheist. In other words, I believe that spirituality entails something more fundamental about us than our theology or lack thereof. Spirituality is that feature of being human concerned with experiencing, living and expanding the best that is within us.

Related to spirituality you will also often encounter the term *spiritual practice.* Spiritual practice is intentional activity engaged in for the purpose of experiencing and integrating spirituality into everyday life. Meditation, prayer, devotional reading, and serving others are examples of spiritual practice. Spiritual practice is the way spirituality grows from an abstract idea into a practical reality in everyday life. Spirituality without spiritual practice becomes barren, an intellectual pastime at best. Spiritual practice nourishes spirituality, enables it to thrive and mature into a dynamic force.

Chapter 3
Awakening

There is a story about the Buddha that goes something like this: shortly after his enlightenment, some people approached him. They recognized that there was something extraordinary about him. They asked him, "Are you a god?" "No," he replied. "Then, are you a magician or a wizard?" Again, he said "No." "Well then, are you a man?" Yet again, the answer was "No." "Well, then, what are you?" they asked. He replied, "I am *awake*."

In this little story is contained the entire essence of spirituality. The questioners began their attempts to understand what they were seeing in this person before them by attributing some special identity to him, a god or a wizard. They kept trying to place him above them in some sense. The Buddha wanted to help his questioners get beyond this idea that he was essentially higher or better than them. Unless you're in a terminal coma, everyone sleeps, everyone has the ability to awaken from sleep. But he goes further to suggest that the awakened man is no longer just a man. When one is awake, one is no longer ordinary.

So, what does awake mean, as applied to the spiritual life? Simply stated, being awake is doing something and knowing that you are doing it, thinking something and knowing that you are thinking it, feeling something and knowing what you are feeling. In the blur of the rushing and multitasking that characterizes our lives, most of the time we are running on automatic pilot. Have you had the experience of walking into a room, having forgotten what you came in for? Have you driven down a stretch of familiar road, arrived at your destination, and with some concern realized you had no recollection of the last five minutes of the trip? In these instances, you may have been awake in a physiological sense but you were certainly not awake in the sense of being conscious.

For most of us, life has become a predictable sequence of routines that are pursued and repeated automatically until there comes a time, often at midlife, when the question arises, "Is this all there is?" This is a wonderful question no matter how painfully wrought, one that emerges from many sources of dissatisfaction. Perhaps the strongest source is that for years we have not been really awake, and this question is the beginning of our rousing from a long slumber. Joseph Campbell characterized it as having gotten to the top of the ladder we were climbing only to discover that we had it against the wrong wall!

The question "Is this all there is?" can occur at any time, not just midlife. The question implies that whatever we have been striving for, and whatever we hoped it would deliver to us, has fallen way short of the mark. We may be left with a feeling of betrayal, that we have bought into a promise that was not delivered on. Usually we have to go through a long series of disappointments before we recognize that we have been "looking for love in all the wrong places" as the song goes. There is a marvelous story about the Sufi Mulla Nasrudin who was famous for tricking people into their own capacity for wisdom:

> Someone saw Nasrudin searching for something
> on the ground.
> 'What have you lost, Mulla?' he asked.
> 'My key,' said the Mulla.

So they both went down on their knees and   looked
for it. After a time the other man asked:
'Where exactly did you drop it?'
'In my own house.'
'Then why are you looking here?'
'There is more light here than inside my own
house.'

> --by permission of Patterson Marsh Ltd.
> on behalf of the Octagon Press

We keep looking in the wrong places because they're the
only places we know to look, but there's an additional
factor.   One of the tendencies that feeds the frenzied
quality of our lives is the value our culture places on setting
and achieving goals and working hard to achieve them,
topped off with a dollop of "idle hands are the devil's
playground." This orientation to life places all good things
in the future. What we don't realize is that the mind does
what it is trained to do.   It develops patterns based on
repetition.   Whether we know we're doing it or not, any
patterns we repeat over time become the mind's way of
perceiving and relating to life. When, day after day, year
after year, we act repeatedly from this future orientation,

we are training our minds to be ever ahead of the present moment. In other words, not present. Therefore, when we arrive at the goal, having trained ourselves all along to look to the future, we find ourselves unable to be fully present and fulfilled. When we're absent from the pursuit, we cannot taste the fruit. We become good at what we train for. After this happens enough times, we raise that very important and wonderful question "Is this all there is?" And, of course, this is more than a casual, philosophical question. It is a question that is usually posed from a vantage of much suffering. Behind it may be a trail of fractured relationships, job dissatisfaction, depression and addiction. There needs to be an answer to this question and it needs to be one that goes beyond therapy. I am a therapist myself and I would never devalue therapy as a way to break unskillful patterns and make positive changes. But, whether they should seek it or not, many people will not try therapy, many people can't afford it, and many people in therapy will never discuss with their therapist the spiritual dimension of life and the resources for change and growth available from it. Spirituality is not the privilege of any elite group. We all need to look for the key in our own house. We just need to know how to look.

Chapter 4
Spare Time . . . , Say What?

When computers first came on the scene, one futurist predicted that someday they would do so much for us that we would have huge tracts of leisure time. Has this proven true in your life? If so, please contact me. I'd like to meet you. What we see instead is both adults in the house working full time or more, the kids pressed into too many activities, and multi-tasking held up as a virtue. The unintended consequences of this lifestyle have spawned a huge stress management industry and have become a major, if not the major, factor in disease. If it were a microbe, the far reaching public health consequences of stress would cause it to be identified as a pandemic.

This way of life is in contrast to the teachings of the spiritual masters throughout history. "Consider the lilies of the field. They toil not; neither do they spin." Our multi-tasking lives, however, define a relationship with time that says "there are only so many minutes in a day." We view time as a quantity that is meted out in the service of our list of activities. It is more like a bank account that we spend down, than a feature of the natural world. We humans have not always had this relationship to time. We were once more adapted to time frames associated with the great rhythms of nature. Cultivating, planting, harvesting and resting were defining features of the cycle of seasons. An example of how out of touch we are with the qualitative aspects of these cycles is the Christmas holiday season. In the northern hemisphere, this is a time when the natural world is in repose, when overt activity of living things has slowed down. Yet, we have turned this time into the most frenetic, frenzied time of the year, 180° out of sync with Nature. I have treated individuals with SAD, so called seasonal affective disorder, and I believe that these individuals for whatever reason have a connection with the natural quality of the season, and that the attempt to override this connection by pursuing business as usual is what creates the depressive trend. Whenever we go against what we feel is a deep or fundamental truth for us, and we persist in this course, we will begin to grieve and find ourselves mourning and may not have a clue as to why. That deep truth may be something our daily routine has kept us so out of touch with that we are sorely perplexed and even frightened by what is happening. Depression of this sort is a call to introspection masquerading as a mood disorder. If we have not developed the capacity to pay attention to our inner lives and treat what dwells there with respect, psyche must, in effect, act as a thief and steal our attention away from business as usual.

What is really a calling to a healthy, restorative introversion therefore turns into an enforced withdrawal. It is as if the "normal" alienation from natural rhythms that we have achieved as "civilized" people has somehow broken down or not been fully achieved for the individual with SAD. Standard treatments are geared toward re-alienation -- light therapy to fool the body into thinking it's not really winter, antidepressants to bar the door to hibernation. While these approaches have the benefit of relieving suffering and restoring a person to normal functioning, they do so at a cost. They pass over the opportunity to engage in a discovery of one's deeper connection to fundamental principles and rhythms of life. In other words, they silence the call from a nascent and deeply personal spirituality. While I acknowledge the value of the judicious use of pharmaceuticals and other symptom-reducing methods, it often seems to me that the treatments we have are themselves examples of the problem for which they are supposed to be the solution.

Most of us in our heart of hearts know that the life that our culture seems to advocate doesn't point the way to happiness. But the train seems to be moving too fast to get off. We can't often tell the difference between the demands life places on us and the demands we place on ourselves. Life just feels like an unrelenting sequence of demands, a checklist that gets longer the more items we check off. Recently the physician I work with shared a book he wanted me to read in pursuit of our setting up a pain management program, suggesting that I look at it in my spare time. "In my what???"

The great difficulty in reclaiming our lives, which I would argue is a big piece of what spirituality is all about, is that we have to begin somewhere, and that somewhere is where we are right now. With not a single spare moment to add anything else, and not one activity that can be given up. Whether this is literally true or not is not the point. It *feels* true, and this feeling is a formidable obstacle to resetting, redirecting our lives.   One cannot be argued into the spiritual life. Perhaps one simply has to be sufficiently fed up with life without it.

Chapter 5
Spiritual Practice

In 1970 the journal, *Science*, broke new cultural ground by publishing an article by Robert Keith Wallace called "The Physiological Effects of Transcendental Meditation." Until then, the spiritual community and the scientific community either avoided each other prejudicially or simply failed to find enough common ground to have a conversation. This landmark study began a dialogue and mutual exploration that has resulted in hundreds of studies published in reputable professional journals. Once regarded by health professionals as, at best, fanciful, at worst, psychosis, meditation is now freely advocated as beneficial for both mental and physical health.

My purpose here is not to list the manifold health benefits of meditation, but to invite a consideration of how important it is from a spiritual vantage. Try a little experiment. Put this book down, close your eyes and for the next five minutes bring all your attention to the sensation of your belly rising and falling with each inbreath and outbreath. Try to attend to nothing else..........What happened? If you are like most people, you were able to attend to three or four breaths and then found yourself thinking about something, noticing an itch or ache in the body, hearing a sound, and so on. If you were to do this exercise for a half-hour, you would be convinced that you have attention deficit disorder! The mind just doesn't want to stay where we put it. Just a short introspective glance and it's easy to be convinced that we are in a more or less perpetual state of internal agitation. *The world we create is a reflection of this.* Everything we experience in the outer world existed first in someone's mind. It is no accident that meditation has been appropriated by psychology and medicine as a *stress management* tool to help calm agitation and anxiety, but even people who don't display flagrant signs of stress will experience this agitated mind phenomenon. What does this mean? The Wallace article proposed that the state of consciousness evoked by meditation constitutes a fourth major state, in addition to waking, dreaming, and deep sleep. It is well known that a person deprived of any of these three states will begin to show pathological mental and/or physical health changes. Is it possible that being deprived of the meditative state also produces pathology that is not recognized as such? In a world where most people do not access the meditative state, the pathology would simply appear as normal, part of the human condition. Dr. Abraham Maslow noted that conventional psychology seems to regard as normal "a state of mild and chronic psychopathology and fearfulness, of stunting and crippling immaturity which we don't notice because most others have this same disease that we have."

Aggression, greed, abuse of the environment, degenerative disease, relationship disharmony, stress disorders, war, poverty....are these and other maladies simply inevitable features of human life or do they have roots in what I call *transcendence deprivation*? In our history as a species there have been individuals such as the Buddha, Jesus, Gandhi and many lesser-known teachers who embodied a higher way of being. The way they invite us to cultivate is not easy, but most would agree that it exemplifies a life experienced as worthwhile and of compassion and respect for one's fellow beings. To be able live life in this way is not something one can sustain for long by acting a certain way. You can't fake it until you make it. Rather, being the best that is within us flows from a certain way of experiencing ourselves and the world. Meditation is a reliable means of embarking on this way.

Even though we know the health benefits of meditation, for most of us it is just one more thing we need to "fit in" to an already over-full schedule. Anything that we add seems to subtract from something else. In the case of meditation, we usually think in terms of time subtracted from sleep, and for many of us leading stressful lives, we don't get enough sleep to begin with. Either we get to bed too late, get up too early, or we sleep fitfully, never sinking into restorative sleep. Or, sleep may be experienced as the longed for respite at the end of a harrowing day, and we're going to give up a piece of this great escape? Jon Kabat-Zinn, Ph.D., founder of the stress reduction clinic at the University of Massachusetts Medical Center, a meditation-based program, notes that "stress reduction is stressful!" He means that changing a pattern of living, even for the best, involves learning new skills, and this requires getting out of one's comfort zone, even if it's an uncomfortable comfort zone!

It has been said that there is a great time paradox with meditation: that by taking the time to meditate you end up having more time. There may be something to this. It makes sense that whatever we do if our starting point is a calm mind will be more efficient and effective than if we start from an agitated mind. With an agitated mind, we make a lot of mistakes and we are likely to get sidetracked. People who have a daily meditation practice over a sustained period will tend to affirm this. But many people never make it to a sustained practice, and there are many reasons for this. Perhaps the main reason is the sheer relentlessness of the responsibilities and time pressure we face, and the unexpressed urgency we may feel to get results NOW. This urgency comes not only from the built up need for relief from stress, but also is reinforced by our culture's mythology of instant gratification -- instant credit, fast food, pills to make the pain go away -- a mythology that feeds our likes, deletes our dislikes, but fails to nourish our souls. In fact, a major component of the stress we experience is that little of the feverish activity that occupies so much of our energy has anything to do with our souls, and the neglect of this deep dimension of life creates a sense that, with all this activity, we are going nowhere.

Solving problems in life comes about in two ways. We either identify the pattern and work on it, adding some new elements and subtracting some others, get insights about how the pattern came about and implement new patterns based on those insights.   It's what most psychotherapy is about. It's about discovering new inner resources, using old resources in new ways, and hopefully in so doing achieving a wiser and more effective way of being in the world. There is another process that does not work directly on problems, but rather awakens a new level of perception. There is an aspect of ourselves that is the silent observer behind the flurry of thoughts, feelings, and activity that constitute all the patterns that we come to think of as who we are and what our life story is.

When we think back to all the different eras of our lives, childhood, adolescence, early adulthood, etc., we can marvel at how different we were in each one. Even in the course of a day, we can be in a very dark mood if faced with a disappointment or frustration and then be ecstatic from the arrival of good news. When you look at it closely, what I call "I" can look pretty discontinuous and variable. And yet, most of us have the underlying sense of being the same person, the same entity from our earliest recollection on into the present moment. What, who, is this underlying sameness? It seems to be present at all times, in the background, the observer, knower or experiencer of all things becoming known and experienced. As we accumulate more knowledge and experience, we become more identified with what we know and what we have experienced, and our awareness of this knower sinks into a deeper background. In our culture, which is ever goal-oriented, full of plans and acting on plans, our fantasy of the future occupies a huge segment of our mental and emotional apparatus. We carry with us increasing amounts of past history and future plans, and come to be defined by both. The underlying observer, knower, experiencer is increasingly obscured by the inertia of history and the sprint into future. Mystics have called this silent observer behind all experience by many names: The Witness, the Self, the Higher Self, God Within, the Inner Christ, the Inner Light, the Source, Being... All terms which suggest a level of being that is deeper, more fundamental, more foundational than the level of daily experience. In addition, they have advocated that accessing this foundational level is the key to cultivating a life that makes sense and that evokes greater degrees of harmony within self and with others. It is as if this deeper Self is our access port to a field that underlies and unifies all existence. Another way of saying it is that it is the Universal within the individual.

But why should we trust what mystics say? In our era of scientific rationalism isn't the way of the mystic an anachronism? Our culture and our era are dominated by a way of defining and exploring reality utilizing the methods of rational thought, scientific experimentation, technology, and sophisticated manipulation of the external world. With these tools we have evoked the greatest understanding of this external world that humankind has ever known. Mystics, on the other hand, have devoted themselves with equal ardor to the exploration, description and understanding of the inner world. Just as scientific rationalist culture has developed modes of inquiry and technologies to understand the external world, mystical culture has developed methods suitable to similar tasks applied to inner reality. Meditation, prayer, rhythmic drumming, psychoactive plants, vision quests, to name but a few methods, have undergone millennia of refinement and the features of the world they have revealed are catalogued in sacred traditions, texts, monastic orders, mystery schools and other institutions that maintain and promote such knowledge. The mystical traditions have a much, much longer history than does the scientific tradition. While contemporary science justifies its claims on the basis of the double-blind experiment, mystical tradition can be seen as having its credentials approved by a several-thousand year longitudinal study.

Because mysticism seems so similar across cultures and times, it can be properly thought of as a spiritual, not just a religious, phenomenon. However, mystics often reside within religious traditions. Most religions have a subset of devotees that is of a decidedly mystical character, such as the Sufis of Islam, the Kabbalists of Judaism, the monastic orders of Christianity and Buddhism, etc. It is not unusual for the mystics to find themselves at odds with the more public domain of their respective religions, because the mystic is forever focused on inner truth, whatever it may be presenting, whereas the religious official is focused at least as much on the preservation and promotion of the religious institution and doctrine.

All this talk of mystics and mysticism is to invite you to consider that what the mystics are absorbed with is increasingly important for us modern people to include in our lives. In the accessing of the foundational level of being that the mystics have so thoroughly explored and elucidated, we begin to build an expanding inner core of peace, vitality, and harmony. While psychological exploration aims at solving problems, spiritual practice involves the tapping of an energy that has always been latent within us, that expands the more it is accessed, that emerges, as it were, with increasing fullness in the middle of our problems and unhealthy patterns, and becomes increasingly the more defining feature of who we are. Another way of saying this, from the health perspective, is that health is not merely the absence of illness. If we can cure all your diseases, does that make you healthy? If we can eliminate your neurosis, does that make you self-actualized? We want more from life than just to function well. We want to feel really alive.

Mystical traditions generally maintain that this foundation or source that we access in meditation can be given a name but that doing so immediately places inappropriate limits on it, and therefore changes it. "The Tao that can be named is not the true Tao", says Lao-Tzu. The Hindus speak of it by saying "neti, neti" (not this, not that). The Jewish Yahweh is actually not a name at all, but the Hebrew letters Y, H, V, H, each of which has an esoteric meaning, which when integrated point to a supreme Reality. It is interesting that when Divinity names itself to Moses, it calls itself "I Am", which corresponds to the Hindu "Sat" (Being). For convenience, I shall henceforth refer to this supreme, foundational level of reality as Being, and the state of consciousness it manifests as, as the Observer. While no term is adequate, in conversation we have to have some way of speaking of this level. I choose Being for two reasons. First, the type of experience that characterizes this level is complete unto itself. It doesn't grasp after anything or reject anything. It doesn't exert a pressure to change into anything else. It doesn't strive to *become* anything. It provides a sense of quietude and contentment with the moment just as it is, and a feeling of inherent harmony within oneself and between oneself and the world. It doesn't have or need a philosophy, theology, or explanation attached to it. When in a moment of Being, it is sufficient just to *Be*. The other reason is the distinction Dr. John Bradshaw makes between human beings and human doings. The frenzied, over-active lives we lead as described in several places in this book define us as human doings. This is a condition where we become defined by the avalanche of activity in our lives rather than by calmness, centeredness, wisdom, and *joie de vivre* which become features of a person in whom Being has been accessed and steadily more infused.

So how do we go about accessing Being, if we feel we cannot make time to do so in a regular meditation practice? Let's just forget for a moment that we *should* be able set aside time every day, that it's not that we can't but that we won't, and all other admonitions from our inner critic that lead us to feel like wimps and failures but never really motivate us to do what we're being shamed for not doing. Let's ask the critic to have a seat in the waiting room. There are many different types of meditation, and the one that will be utilized here is often given the name *mindfulness*. Mindfulness can be defined as paying attention, on purpose, to whatever arises in awareness in the present moment, without identifying with any of it. Let's unpack this definition. *Paying attention, on purpose*: in meditation, there is both attention and intention. It is not spacing out. It is also not thinking about, figuring out, or contemplating. It is not an intellectual exercise, even a lofty spiritual intellectual exercise. It is, rather, a deliberate, conscious decision to be awake, alert and receptive...*to whatever arises in awareness in the present moment.* What arises may be thoughts, emotions, body sensations, sounds, sights, smells, tastes. *In the present moment* means that we give our purposeful attention to what is arising right now. *Without identifying with any of it*: If we are thinking about how someone said something offensive to us a few hours ago, and are feeling hurt and angry and we begin planning and rehearsing what we are going to say to them next time we see them, we are *identified* with this stream of thought and the emotions that proceed from it. We are not in the present moment. One line of thinking has carried us into the past -- the memory of the offensive remark. The other has carried us into the future -- the planning for revenge. And we are caught up in the drama of it. We are not free. Being in the present moment, and not identifying with what is arising, comes from taking the seat of the Observer, and the Observer is the face of Being. This thought, that feeling, this body sensation, that smell, are all like boats sailing down the river as I sit on the beach and watch them sail past. I may note "thinking," "sad", "itching" and "sweet" as I observe each one arising, but I am just the Observer, paying attention, on purpose, receptive, but allowing each one to be what it is without attempting to change it in any way. I observe each boat as it passes, without swimming out and climbing on board any of them. If I find that my purposeful awareness has temporarily weakened, I've already regained awareness, right? So I take a breath, observing "in" and "out", and return to the present moment and what is arising in it. If I find that my mind is wandering a lot I might hear a thought like "I'll never get the hang of this" or "this may work for some people but not for me" or any of a thousand judgments on myself or the practice, in which case I simply note "judging" or "thinking" to myself and let the next moment bring what it will bring.

Each time we return to the present moment, to the position of Observer, we are establishing ourselves in Being, for that moment. It might be nice if we could turn on a switch and be there all the time, but beware of pressuring yourself to have "good" meditations, because this is one sure-fire way to get discouraged and stop the practice. The fact is, you don't have to be "on target" every single moment. What we get better at with practice is not so much always being focused, but recognizing when we've wandered.

Take a minute now to think about, and even write down so you don't have to trust your memory, all of the different times of the day where you have to stop and wait, for whatever reason. Some of my favorites are: stopped at a red light; waiting in the teller line at the bank; waiting for the telephone voice menu to get to the option I want; waiting for the computer to boot up; waiting for my wife to get ready to go somewhere with me. Estimate how much time these incidents might add up to in a day. When I ask people, most estimate a half hour to an hour a day, sometimes more. What do we usually do with moments? Generally, we either space out or stress out. Either we go unconscious or we get all worked up about the problems we imagine this delay *is going to* cause us. Either way, we are not present. Yet here, in these moments, is the ideal time to engage in mindfulness. We're not subtracting time from any other important activity or agenda. The only "demand" we're placing on ourselves is to take time already set before us to engage in something liberating!

My favorite personal example of this occurred several years ago. I had overslept and was racing to the office for a 9:00 appointment. Parking was very limited at the building in which my office was located, and as I pulled into the parking lot, already unconscious due to rushing and stressing, I saw that someone had parked in my space, which meant that I would have to back up, turn around, and park in the city lot a long way away, making me even later. I was furious. I was going to put a note on the person's windshield letting them know in no uncertain terms how unacceptable this was. No, on second thought, I was going to have the SOB towed! By some miracle, in the midst of this inner rampage the thought occurred to me to engage mindfulness. Interestingly, the first thing I became mindful of was a self-righteous insistence that in this situation I had earned the right to be mindless, that is, stuck in the suffering of being enraged at the great injustice that had been done to me and in the completely justified plan to add to someone else's suffering! I then began to focus on my breathing, or, more accurately, on the sensations created in my nose, chest and abdomen as the breath moved in and out, and made a decision to deepen the breathing, having observed that my breath had become shallow and rapid. Observing the breath seemed to bring my attention more into the present moment. I was aware of the sensations of the breath, of anger, of a tightness in my stomach and temples, of thoughts of revenge. As I continued over the next few seconds to become more mindful, I also became aware of the sky, which was cloudless, of the sensation of warmth and humidity in the air, of the texture and color of the gravel of the parking lot, and of the other vehicles in the lot. As I increasingly assumed the position of Observer, I was noticing a calmness setting in. I then noticed, that over in the unmarked, visitors section of the parking lot was an open space that I had completely missed! A thought flashed through my mind of a bumper sticker I had recently seen" "Only visiting this planet." I became aware of the intention to drive into the parking space, the movement and pressure of my foot on the accelerator, the hand-over-hand lifting, moving, placing of hands on the steering wheel to guide the car into the space, the intention to apply the brake, the lifting movement of the foot from the accelerator pedal, the placing of it on the brake pedal, the application of pressure, the shifting scenery as the car made the turn into the open space, the sounds of the tires on the gravel...in short, the moment-to-moment awareness of the inner and outer sensations and accompanying thoughts and feelings arising in each present moment. Notice that this awareness did not exclude the anger and the thoughts of revenge. It did not involve trying to push them away or to change them in any way. Rather, it was the switching on of the element of *awareness*, the decision to shift from identifying with the raging storm of planning and anger to identifying with the *Observer* of these things and of all else arising in the present moment that changed everything. One of the thoughts I became aware of as I was beginning to experience some calmness was how *unconscious* I was when I was identified with all the emotion and thinking that was going on -- my vision was so tunnelized that I wasn't even aware that there was an open parking space within easy reach!

There is a subtle aspect of mental functioning that receives little attention in modern psychology. There is seeing and there is the knowing of seeing. There is hearing and the knowing of hearing. There is thinking and the knowing of thinking, and so on. In this example, the eyes were seeing the empty parking place -- it wasn't that far away! But the knowing of the seeing was absent. How many times have you looked all over the house for something and on the fourth pass found it where you had already looked? When we're rushing around, agitated because we need to find those keys because we're already late, our eyes see but our knowing what we are seeing, our awareness, our *Observer* has not been invited to the viewing! How many times in my life have I been blind to possibilities because I was mindless, unconscious, so totally fixed on some agenda that was making me suffer but that I was fully convinced was the only right way to proceed? Sobering.

As I finished parking and proceeded into the building, I made a point to continue being mindful as I walked, ascended the stairway, opened the door, and so forth and by the time I was fully situated in the office I decided not to have the person towed. It would have taken more time and thereby added to my stress by making me late for my appointment, and it would have revived some strong negative emotion. What would be the point in doing that? Now, let me point out something important here. It would have been justified and appropriate to call the tow truck. Mindfulness does not advocate that it is OK to allow someone to step across your boundaries, or that it is not OK to take corrective action once this has occurred. What mindfulness does accomplish in such instances is a much more clear-headed and clear-hearted evaluation of the situation and of the relative merits of different possible courses of action. If corrective action of some sort is decided upon, coming from a calm mind and heart allows the action to be chosen with wisdom and to be executed with compassion. This is of a very different quality for both the giver and the receiver of corrective action than that delivered from an agitated mind and an angry heart. Such action damages not only the receiver but the executor of such behavior.

Think of some examples of similar situations in which you have behaved mindfully, and mindlessly. Then, over the next few days make it a point to pay attention in situations in which you are required to stop and wait, or where your plans get interrupted in some fashion. Instead of giving in to the usual chain of reactions, use each situation to shift into the mode of mindfulness. Here are some handy clues:

1) Use the discomfort you feel when you have to stop, or when your plans are interrupted, as a cue to begin paying attention.

2) To help shift away from the usual cascade of negative emotion and negative thinking, begin to focus on your breath, specifically, on the physical sensations of the air coming in and out of the nose and/or mouth, and the rising and falling of the belly, chest, and shoulders.

3) Notice whether the breath has become shallow or limited and allow it to slow down and deepen.

4) When you have balanced your breathing, begin to just take note of what you are experiencing in the moment -- the thoughts going through your mind, the emotions, the body sensations, the sights and sounds in your

surroundings. Allow yourself to become the Observer of everything that is arising.

5) Whenever you become aware that you have stumbled back onto the avalanche of feverish thinking and negative emotion, gently bring your attention back to the breath and then back to awareness of what is arising in the present moment, allowing yourself to notice the inner and the outer features of the moment. Bring yourself back to the moment as often as the time allows.

6) When the light changes, when the bank line moves ahead, see if you can continue to practice mindfulness as you drive down the road or make your deposit. See how long you can extend your mindfulness into the rest of life.

What is being described here is using time that is already on the horizontal line to "go vertical". It is about taking time that is already there but being seriously misspent and utilizing it in a way that opens a channel to the spiritual dimension. At the very least, this practice will produce increasing levels of calmness in situations where tension predominated. But, more importantly, each activation of the observing consciousness strengthens the connection between the spiritual and the mundane levels of life. It's as if these two dimensions are separated by a path full of debris, the debris being the fretful thoughts and emotions, the rushing, the planning and obsessing. Each moment spent in mindfulness is a broom sweeping away some of the debris. What begins as a single moment of being five percent less stressed than the last time the cash register in my line broke down, becomes in time, maybe not much time, a moment in which I experience some pleasure in having slowed to a stop. A moment to breathe, to relax, to accept the world and myself exactly as we are for now. Even, perhaps, to feel some compassion, not only for the poor fool at the cash register, but for the poor fool inside me that is still trying to get me and the situation to hurry the hell up. In this radical acceptance, perhaps I begin to get an inkling of what is meant by *spiritual*.

Chapter 6
Spiritual Modesty

The process just described doesn't seem very lofty, very mystical, very exciting. There is no ecstasy, no extrasensory perception, nothing that's going to make interesting conversation at the coffee break. We tend to have picked up the view that spirituality is supposed to produce experiences that are dramatically discontinuous from our everyday lives. Certainly this can happen. There are many stories of people experiencing extraordinary things. Near death experiences, visions, premonitions, prophetic dreams to name but a few. For the most part, these extraordinary experiences happen to people unbidden or as a part of an apparent gift or talent. There remains the question of how such experiences are to be integrated into the business of everyday life. Will the boss understand that I was too busy having visions of the end times to come to work? One of my clients began having spontaneous visionary experiences identical with those reported by tribal shamans. She was befriended by a bear who took on the role of a spiritual protector and advisor. Primal cultures often include the concept of the Power Animal in their spiritual systems in exactly this capacity. For my client, a devoted Christian, this represented a major challenge. It was additionally challenging because the ongoing unfolding of these visions were, from an everyday life vantage, untimely. Her family faced major financial stresses that were requiring her to seek employment outside the home. The energy required to understand and give attention to new developments in her spiritual life seemed to pull her away from the down-to-earth demands she was facing. The more dramatic spiritual experiences often pose this dilemma. The bulk of our work recently has been to begin to achieve integration between developments in her spiritual life and the requirements of her mundane life.

In cases where an extraordinary ability or experience manifests, there is huge disruption because the person's daily life routines have not been constructed to include and sustain such a radically new way of being in the world. Such a spontaneous spiritual mobilization can put one on the fast track of spiritual development, and many people hear of these more dramatic experiences and begin to hope for or even try to evoke them. Most traditions with which I am familiar regard this as an unwise practice. Extraordinary abilities require the simultaneous cultivation of extraordinary wisdom and maturity, a requirement added to a psyche already stretched to its limits by the powerful experience itself.

Spiritual practice such as the one being presented here takes as a starting point a person's daily experience and simply adds the element of awareness to what is already going on. Awareness, the shifting of one's standpoint from the action to the Observer, changes the situation but always in a gentle way. This is its immediate, short-term effect. Over the long term, the repeated shift into this Observer mode allows awareness as a feature of Being to accumulate, expand and become a more established and stable feature of a person's makeup. It is said that as this feature grows, along with it often come heightened abilities and sensitivities such as extrasensory perception, healing, visions and so on, but these are by-products of a growing and stabilized spiritual practice. They rest on a firm foundation of wisdom, maturity and understanding and

therefore are less likely to destabilize an individual's daily
life or be put to ill use.

People who have been gifted with special spiritual talents
or who have had such things disruptively thrust upon them
still need, or perhaps have an especially pressing need, for
a spiritual practice that grounds them in everyday life and
allows a bridge to be built between the new world that has
opened to them and the one that we have to live in every
day. Whether we are stopped at a red light or having a
vision of a Power Animal, what renders the experience
valuable is the quality of our awareness in that moment.
With dim awareness, with unstable awareness, any
experience can have little value. A stop light can be
nothing more than an interruption and a visionary
experience can cause our daily life to derail. It is only with
the cultivation of awareness, of Being, of the Observer that
any experience, no matter how objectively mundane or
sublime, can be the vehicle for awakening. This is a point I
want to underscore and overemphasize. To awaken, to
grow in wisdom, to mature spiritually, is not about
accumulating dramatic experiences. It is about waking up,
being present, about touching the material of everyday,

mundane, regular, down to earth experience with awareness. I was at a meditation retreat where we were practicing walking meditation. We were barefoot, walking slowly and deliberately, back and forth over a span of maybe ten to fifteen feet. The idea was, as already described, to walk with awareness of walking -- of the intention to lift the foot, of actually lifting, moving, placing, etc. What happens as awareness begins to expand in such exercises is that it begins to take in ever more subtle perceptions, like turning up the magnification on a microscope. I began to become really fascinated by the sensation of the ground under my feet. There were patches of different types of grass and clover and each had its own particular texture and warmth. Each absorbed and reflected the heat of the sun differently. As I became more fascinated by these discoveries, I also noticed that I was becoming very peaceful inside and also a feeling of joy that seemed to have a vibratory quality to it physically. All of this coming from walking and increasingly fuller degrees of knowing of walking! At some point it occurred to me the sheer pleasure I was experiencing in this most absurdly simple experience was greater than anything I had experienced on my Harley, which cost a whole lot more and was much more dangerous.

We spend a lot of money and put a lot of time and energy into things that we feel we must have in order to feel fulfilled.   What I became aware of in this walking meditation is that, when we have little awareness, we feel we must have a lot of stimulation in our lives.   When we have a lot of awareness, we can get by with very little, because the little we have is quite enough to keep us occupied!

Chapter 7
Just Show Up
Journal Entry 3/20/06

I went for a walk this morning and was trying to let my attention open to the sights, sounds, fragrances and so forth, bringing my awareness back to this present moment experience whenever my mind began anticipating and planning the events of the day ahead. I was about a third of the way around the lake when I noticed that my awareness had definitely shifted. I was aware, taking it all in, but it was like Awareness was the main thing and I was contained in it, along with the lake, the trees, the geese and ducks, the air, the thoughts that were streaming through my head, an so on. I can't even phrase it as "I experienced x, y, z" because "I" seemed to be one of several objects in this field of Awareness, which I'm capitalizing, I guess, in order to emphasize that Awareness seemed to be the main thing happening, not just the center of things but everything from the center on out. Impossible to describe.

One of the most striking features of this event was the shifting of the sense of myself from being the center of the experience to being merely one of the participants in it. I have to wonder if this way of experiencing life were to become more frequent, it couldn't help but make one's connections with other people and the world at large feel very real and personal, as if contained by an overarching presence.

So how did this happen to me? How does this happen to anyone? There doesn't seem to be a way to make it happen as a result of some mechanical or reproducible process. On the other hand, it did happen when I was practicing mindfulness on my walk. I've done this walk many times, mindfully and mindlessly. Why this time? Recent studies of meditation suggest that when the mind is quiet, electrical activity increases in areas of the brain associated with expansive awareness. Like a cloud cover on a rainy day obscuring all but a small portion of sunlight, the agitated mind clouds over the inner light of Awareness that is always potentially the clarifying and unifying quality of life.

When the experience began to fade I found myself wanting to bring it back, which didn't work, so I just observed the wanting and the not working of it. What began and ended as a mindful walk around the lake became briefly a spiritual experience of Oneness. It's hard not to be driven to figure out exactly what I did to make that happen, but I've been through that. Just show up, Nourse. Just show up.

Chapter 8
Spirituality and Relationship

The stage on which our most significant hopes, dreams, projects and conflicts play themselves out is the interpersonal relationship. This is true in whatever the relationship context -- employer/employee, friendship, business relationship or spouse.   In no other situation does it become more apparent how readily we make our happiness dependent upon factors external to us, and therefore set ourselves up for suffering. Not to mention the suffering created for the other person, who finds that she has unwittingly been fit into our agenda as needing to follow a certain script in order to meet our requirements for happiness. And what exacting writers, producers and directors we are! Most if not all the time we are not even aware we are doing this with each other. *Aware*. There's that concept again.   Without awareness, we stumble through relationship on automatic pilot comprised of habit patterns learned from parents, relatives and other people who have themselves inherited many generations' worth of conditioning.

There have been many books written about how to improve your relationships and I see no need to repeat the good work that's already out there on active listening, I-messages, reflecting, conflict resolution, and so on. There are many volumes that describe how we project onto others the unfinished business left over from conflicts with parents and other authority figures. This book is about using what we are given in everyday life as an opportunity for awakening, and, in doing so, to enhance our experience of everyday life and lend it a sense of being sacred ground. Relationship is such a huge part of everyday life, there must be a huge capacity for awakening there!

When conflict arises in a relationship, there also arises a sense of urgency. When there is little or no awareness present, this urgency will cause a person to press forward with his case, in an attempt to make the other person see things his way. Of course, the other person is doing the same, so things can escalate pretty quickly. If an individual has few skills for dealing with conflict, the situation can even degenerate into physical violence, but just at the level of the spoken word, raised voices, sarcasm, threats of various sorts can all be hurtful and do great damage. The tragedy is that these instinctive and unskillful actions accomplish exactly the opposite of what we want, which is to be heard, understood, valued and to move forward together. In working with interpersonal conflict one of the first things I tell people is "almost always, you can buy yourself some time." This urgency about getting the other person to come around is the great enemy of growth and harmony in relationship, not to mention how it quashes any opportunity for spiritual development. I want to talk about two factors in buying time that are of the utmost importance in the process of awakening in the midst of relationship.

The first factor is the cooldown effect, which has been known about forever and is the basis of the "bite your lip" and "count to ten" prescriptions of folk psychology. This is all about taking time to allow fear, hurt, anger and whatever other emotions may be fueling the sense of urgency a chance to subside. When the temperature indicator on the dashboard is in the red zone and jets of steam are escaping from under the hood, this is the time to pull onto the shoulder and for now just simply let the engine cool down. It is not the time to keep driving in hopes of completing whatever agenda seemed so important, and it isn't time to unscrew the radiator cap. There are some misconceptions going around about "getting it all out" and "blowing off steam" that need to be corrected. There are some psychological techniques that include the opportunity to engage in emotion-release, but it is important to understand that these techniques are carefully and caringly structured and employed in a safe and supportive setting, and utilized for purposes of healing traumas. Intense emotion release is not a prescription for daily living. I have worked with many people who have said to me "I thought you shrinks tell people to just get it all out"; or, "I'm just a very emotional person. I blurt it out and then I'm done with it. That's just the way I deal with things and my husband should learn not to take it personally." In the first instance, we shrinks *don't* prescribe just getting it all out, if that means spewing out your rage on whomever happens to be unlucky enough to have crossed you or your path at the time. There is a major difference between telling someone how you feel and launching emotional missiles at them. In the case of blurting it out and being done with it, at first glance this makes some sense. It's well known that stuffed emotion leads to a host of problems, both mental and physical. But is it true that, when it comes to strong emotions, the only choices we have are to blurt them or to stuff them? I'll return to this question in a minute.

How do we buy ourselves time? Pretty simple. Here are some key phrases that you can use or put into your own words:

- I'm starting to feel pretty upset now and I need to cool down before I talk about it.

- I've heard what you said and I need time to take it in and think about it.

- If I talk to you about this now, I'm afraid I'll say something hurtful and I don't want to do that, so I need to think about it and talk later when I'm calmer.

- I appreciate your telling me this, and I need some time to think about it before I tell

you what I'm feeling because I want to be
clear.

These examples buy you time so that when you do get back
to the person (and it's important that you do!), you're
responding rather than reacting. Anything you say will
have a greater chance of being spoken effectively and be
better received because you will be coming from a calm,
rather than an agitated, mind frame. In addition, when
you tell someone you're going to think about it and get
back to them, you're telling them that you take them and
what they have said seriously, i.e., that you value them and
the relationship you have with them enough to reflect upon
their concerns and respond to them in a respectful way.
It's hard for someone to stay agitated and angry if you've
just given them this affirmation. If, however, they're
itching for a fight ("no, I want an answer NOW!!!"):

- If I talk now, this is going to become an
    argument. Do you really want that?

- Do you want to work this out, or do you want an
    argument? If you want to work this out,

> I need to take some time to settle down so I
> can hear what you're saying more clearly.

What's tough about this is that you probably feel completely justified in striking back. The other person is being ridiculous and stubborn, it's not fair that they're blurting out their feelings and I'm playing the pacifist, why do I have to be the one who does this the "right" way? The answer is that this is the umpteenth version of the same old argument and leads nowhere but to more pain, and someone has to start doing it differently or this will just be argument #156. One of my clients realized that during his forty years of marriage he and his wife had the same six arguments over and over, and he had the idea of numbering each one. That way they could just scream at each other "NUMBER 4!!!!" and spare themselves the details. You can resist it or resent it, but the one who has the most awareness, who can see a different way, has to be the one who makes the first move. Gandhi's dictum "Be the change you wish to see in the world" is exactly about this.

Having bought yourself some time, what do you do? The second factor in buying time could be called the mindfulness effect. This is using the conflicts in relationship in the same manner as those times when you are forced to stop and wait. To be mindful in the midst of a conflict, to gradually become mindful earlier in the conflict, to develop the capacity to be mindful at the earliest signals of conflict on the horizon, is to master a very important part of the art of living. When we become aware that a relationship encounter is headed in a painful direction, we have already begun to practice mindfulness. If we can use this awareness as a signal to allow this awareness to begin to expand, we begin to occupy the seat of the Observer as I have already spoken of it, and as we come to rest increasingly in this position, we become less and less identified with the fight, with having to win it, with having to make the other person see it our way. At the same time, what started as an interpersonal conflict becomes an opportunity for touching and expanding that quality of Being that has such a peaceful yet enlivening influence in our lives.

You might begin by getting clear with yourself exactly how you know when there is a problem coming up between you and someone else. It's always good to check in with your body and your breath. Almost always, when tension begins to come up between people, you can identify some change in sensation somewhere in the body, and you can notice that your breathing becomes limited. Body sensations often consist of a tightness in the neck or shoulders, or a feeling of vague pressure in the interior of the body, discomfort in the area of the stomach, increased heart rate, to name a few. Breathing may become shallow, more rapid, or there may be a tendency to hold the breath. Get to know what your internal cues are that tell you you're stepping into a conflict. And then allow your awareness of the moment you're in to expand, to include emotions that are arising in you, and any stream of thought that may be moving through. One of the really interesting things to note is the inner thought commentary that is going on during a conflict. You may become aware that a whole set of interpretations of what the other person is saying is taking place, and a rehearsal of your comeback or counterattack. From the position of Observer, just allow yourself to breathe, to be aware, to sit with, and as much as possible not resist what is coming up. Even if you resist, see if you can also become aware of resistance and what it feels like. Let yourself be aware of the other person and the physical setting the situation is taking place in. Be aware of the internal pressure you keep feeling to jump into the argument whole hog, and then breathe with it, stay with it. When you find yourself veering toward identifying with the angry feelings, the hurt feelings, the thought stream, or whatever is arising, gently bring yourself back to the Observer. As you continue to work with yourself in this fashion, you will find that none of these inner phenomena stay the same. They all have a beginning, a middle, and an end, so to speak. I can sit with my anger, breathe with it, note where I feel it in my body, note that thoughts go along with it, and it will run its course for now and settle down. I have not suppressed it; neither have I acted it out. I have therefore not used it to do violence to the other person or to myself. Touching whatever arises inside with this observing awareness respects its place in the inner ecology of my experience.

What happens as I allow this mindful attention to expand is usually greater calm, centering and clarity, and the possibility that I might make use of the feelings and thoughts that have come up in a more skillful way. Anger is not destructive when I can use it as a signal that something is happening that feels unacceptable to me, rather than as a weapon to strike back. The short-term effect of viewing our relationships through the lens of mindfulness is that conflict can be reduced. Psychologist Robert Pennington of Resource International, Inc., has referred to this as "catching the snowflake before it becomes an avalanche." Conflict in relationship is so much like this. It begins with a thought or interpretation of what someone means when they say X. If I interpret X as meaning something negative, and believe unswervingly that this is NOT an interpretation but truth itself, then this interpretation will generate a negative emotion such as fear, shame, anger or rage (or all of the above), which will cascade into either retaliation or stuffing. In the case of retaliation, overt warfare will break out. In the case of stuffing, covert war is waged (the silent treatment, emotional withdrawal, psychosomatic illness). Mindfulness offers a third alternative which neither fights nor flees, neither attacks nor represses, but which treats both the inner and the outer dimensions of the situation with respect, literally allowing both people and the situation breathing room. Letting the snowflake be just the snowflake, or, if it has become a snowball, at least not throwing it. The unanticipated positive side effect is nothing less than having had one more dip into the state of Being and all the benefits it confers.

In buying time, and then in shifting perspective from attacker, counter-attacker or victim to that of Observer, we allow a latent potential for peace within us a chance to begin to surface. It's not so much that we make peace as that we clear the way for peace. The work involved is refusing the commands of our impulses to press forward into action, no matter how justified it may feel. Each moment of conflict in a relationship presents a choice between being right and being true. In mindlessness I can become so lost in pressing my case that I fail to see or hear what impact I am having on you. I may "win" the argument, but I have just lost a piece of the relationship.

If this happens enough, there will be no relationship left. I will also have lost an opportunity to allow my own awareness to expand into a larger perception of reality, which includes not only the validity of my argument, but also the impact of my behavior on the other person, and of other possibilities that cannot be seen when I am trapped in the tunnel of my own insistent agenda. I know this is difficult. Conflict in relationships can trigger unresolved wounds and their resulting emotions from early childhood, and a marriage can then become the staging ground for righting an ancient wrong rather than solving a contemporary problem. The force of these unconscious dynamics is powerful, and may require psychotherapy to resolve. Whether this is the case or not, the choice to invoke mindfulness as conflict is building is a choice to shift from an insistence upon being right to being true – true to the value of the relationship that I have committed myself to, to the possibility that more is at stake than my own position, and to the potential for spiritual growth that comes when I am willing to sit with the tension and for now *not know* what to do with it.

Fidelity in our contemporary understanding of marriage has become reduced to a legalistic notion of sexual loyalty, but it is a good deal more than that. It is both a commitment and a devotion to a higher reality, an undefined and invisible reality that is greater than the two individual realities that comprise it. Understood in this way, fidelity is present when I can know and tell you what I feel without attacking you, know and tell you what I think without coercing you, disagree with you totally without behaving disrespectfully toward you, because, above all I value you, myself, and the relationship too highly to do otherwise. When I do otherwise, I am having an affair with one of my old lovers – fear, coercion, manipulation, rage, self-pity, self-righteousness.   I'm ducking out on the relationship and finding comfort in an old familiar one. To buy time, to become mindful, to be willing to not know for now, to breathe and sit with every thought and feeling that is arising without having to change or act on them in any way for now, is to give this larger reality of the relationship an opportunity to come into focus, just as the larger reality of Being is emerging within.

If "no time" is one of the arguments against adopting any intensive spiritual practice, how much time would you estimate you spend engaged in fighting with your significant other, always getting the same result? Here is an opportunity to shift from mindless, repetitive infidelity to a love that is true! Traditionally it has been held that celibate monasticism is the surest path to enlightenment, but it may be in our age that intimacy and its inevitable conflicts offer an untapped reservoir of spiritual possibility. To tap that reservoir we must, as in other contexts, use time already present but previously misused as a point of departure into new potentials.

Chapter 9
Journal Entry
April 15, 2006

The sun has just broken through the clouds of a gray Sunday morning, and the sky is rapidly clearing. The breeze stages a contest between the chill of the recent rainy morning and the warmth of the emerging afternoon. To my right outside the window is an explosion of color wrought by the efforts of God and my wife Judith and a touch of sweat equity from me. I feel content. Yesterday I did not. I was out of sorts, hypersensitive. It was one of those days that felt like nothing was going the way I wanted. Judith and I were at odds with each other. Among other things, I felt in conflict between two values I hold: to be able to adapt to, relax with, open to the immediate experience rather than rejecting it or trying to impose my own agenda, vs. being assertive, setting boundaries, taking responsibility for what I want. Back and forth, feeling passive and put upon on the one hand, and angry and wanting to exert control on the other. It makes for a strange mix if I feel stuck between these opposites. I end up going along with everything but with an attitude. And I recognize this is something that goes all the way back. I don't know how far that is, but all the way is what it feels like. I remember a picture my mother took of my dad and I at a picnic stop on the way to Minnesota one summer. He has a forced half smile and I am frowning and scratching my head, which is cocked to one side. I asked him once what was going on in that picture and he said "you were probably griping about something." All the way back. I was also aware of a huge temptation to fly into blame. I'm in this lousy mood because you did X and you didn't do Y and you don't respect my needs, and on and on. One of the hardest things in this life is just to know what the hell is really going on, much less what to do about it if you manage to find out.

When I was in training for Chinese medicine, one of my teachers noted that Chinese diagnosis was a little like a weather report. The patient has dampness in the Spleen, wind-stroke, heat in the five hearts, etc. The weather metaphor may feel uncannily precise if you spend any time sitting with eyes closed just watching what goes on in mind and body. These moods of the past two days feel just like weather systems. A cold front blows in and turns everything dark and gray for awhile, and then a warm front moves in and the sun enlivens everything in view as well as the viewer. And do I have any control over this? Not really, not any more than I can make it stop raining. I sat in mindful contemplation of the then current mood and noticed that there are many thoughts buzzing around like I just mentioned -- I'm not getting to do what I want, I'm having to adapt to the other person too much, there won't be any time left this weekend for me to have some quiet, blah, blah, blah. Does the mood create the thoughts or is it the other way around? And what would I do with the answer to that question? Would it help me change how I'm feeling? Or is the feeling of pressure to change what I'm feeling making it harder to feel anything else, because I'm tensing up against what I'm feeling, and I can actually feel this in my body and my breathing?

It's a whole lot easier to blame the other person. Even if I can't convince them they're wrong, I get to be right in my own mind. Even if I don't feel understood and valued, it's because they don't know how good I really am. And even though that doesn't make me feel good, feeling bad is just the price I pay for being with someone who isn't perceptive enough or sensitive enough to know who they're dealing with.

The self that has this number running has a full time job just keeping up with its own maintenance schedule. In this self's world, the world and the people and events in it have the power to determine how I feel, what kind of day I'm having and how I see them and myself. I have to do my damnedest to maximize my pleasure, shield myself against pain, and I have to make this happen by getting everyone and everything around me to behave correctly. It's exhausting.

> *Now you are tangled up in others, and have forgotten what you once knew, and that's why everything you do has some weird failure in it.*
>
> *--Kabir*

No matter how good I get at making this self's agenda happen, I feel my life has some weird failure in it, because there is a knowing in me that this little self with its whole elaborate program is barking up the wrong tree. So what is this knowing? From time to time in mindfulness I have had the experience of becoming very calm and at the same time alert to everything around and within me. It's that witnessing or observing awareness that is conscious of everything going on but not taken over by any of it. In another sense, it feels like an expansive container in which everything inside and outside is taking place. I can understand why one would be tempted to give it an exalted name like the Higher Self because we need to refer to it in conversation somehow. Whatever one chooses to call it, it seems to be a whole lot bigger than the little self and its feverish pursuit of self-justification, self-promotion and self-preservation.

I once heard someone talking about Grace and they were saying that you can't make it happen but you can prepare yourself to receive it, and this is one of the ways I have come to view spiritual practice. "Receive" is the operative idea. If I get greedy about it so that I'm practicing with the agenda of gittin' me summa dat Grace, it ain't happenin'. I may know what I ultimately want, but the assignment for this moment is to show up in my own movie.

Awareness that contains and embraces joy and sadness, pleasure and pain, contentment and suffering. What might it be like to live from that place? What would my world, *the* world, be like if that were the operative mode of human life? If the experience of our own little worlds weren't enough, the media pummels us daily with overwhelming scenarios of human suffering and invitations to live in worry and fear, as well as false assurances that if we buy this car or eat this yogurt or wear these jeans, we will be able to get free from all of it. It can sometimes seem like the human species has skewed off onto some evolutionary side rail that is headed to a dead end. Resting in mindfulness, one sees how little influence one initially has over one's thoughts. The world as it is has been fashioned by minds that have never looked inside long enough to have realized this fact, and these undisciplined minds create the world we know. A mind that is on this kind of automatic pilot cannot help but create and maintain a world that is run by the engines of fear, greed and aggression. It would seem that the only way open to human beings is the cultivation of a state of being that is in some sense larger than the warring states that battle for the collective soul.

In Alcoholics Anonymous there is the recognition that, for recovery to begin, one must admit that one is powerless over alcohol, and that one must also enlist one's Higher Power if the venture is to succeed. There is a profound humility in this that one also experiences in mindfulness, seeing how initially powerless one is to control one's own inner experience and the outer reality of one's life that emanates from it. Whether the process of cultivating awareness begins from some sort of hitting bottom, or just from really seeing in a clear way the random and chaotic excursions of the mind, the task of life shifts from pursuit of pleasure and avoidance of pain to a deeper desire to understand and relate to one's life and Life itself in a wiser and more compassionate way.

The fact that it is possible in spiritual practice to open to what is present, to hold it in awareness, and that this simple act begins to transform us suggests, certainly, that this is something that human beings are wired for. We arrive from the factory with this feature. It's on the hard drive waiting to be accessed. Cultivation of awareness certainly implies that there is work involved, that ground has to be prepared and planting has to take place. But the seeds that are planted know what they have to do. Our cultivation makes it possible for them to follow their genetic mandates more fully and effectively. Spiritual practice doesn't create awareness, but allows it to grow more fully and effectively. This is good news, for it suggests that within each of us is a genetic blueprint for a more sublime life, should we decide to make a place for it to gestate and be born. Could this be one meaning of Christmas? The Light of the World, Enlightenment, comes about when one stable-izes one's inner world so that this latent capacity for awareness has a window through which to enter one's life. It's not about Jesus, or the Buddha, or any prophet or avatar or savior, but about what they have illustrated for us regarding our own birthright.

Chapter 10
A Place of Refuge

Our strategy for developing simple spirituality has focused on two scenarios that are universal in modern life: those times when we are forced to stop and wait, and those times when we experience challenges in interpersonal relationships. We have seen how both can become transformed from problem zones into sacred ground, arenas for awakening through the tool of mindfulness. We have thus seen how spiritual practice can begin to develop in the midst of, and using the material found in, ordinary everyday life.

The remainder of this book will be devoted to presenting some tools that can provide support to spiritual practice. In keeping with our premise that spirituality can begin to grow using nothing more than time heretofore misspent, these tools are offered as encouragements for those who are curious about and are now willing to find time for some additional practices. They are in no way substitutes for the core practice, nor are they requirements. They should be seen as reinforcements of the core practice to be employed as possible and as desired.

In the western legal system the codes of conduct are called laws. In old Hawai`i's legal system, they were called kapu. The Hawaiian system had a provision not found in the western system, known as the pu`uhonua or place of refuge. If one had violated kapu or was otherwise the subject of pursuit by authorities, if he were able to reach a place of refuge, he was in safe haven and could not be apprehended. These were not easy places to reach and one who found his way to a pu`uhonua was considered to have found favor with the gods and was put through purification rituals and processes by the kahuna (spiritual practitioners) and then released as free and cleansed.

How often do we find ourselves feeling as if we are being pursued, whether by deadlines at work, financial demands, relationship and family crises? Even worse, the inner demons of self-condemnation either take us by surprise or easily run us down, in both senses of the phrase. The practice of mindfulness is a pu`uhonua. From the vantage of Being, of the Observer, we can witness the forces that pursue us gathering all around, but they are not allowed in. We can touch them with our awareness, but they cannot seize hold of us from this place. Does this mean we spend all our time in the place of refuge? With practice, with the gradual accumulation of experiences of Being, perhaps the world becomes our place of refuge. Meanwhile, we can awaken in this or that moment, using Being as the place of refuge to become peaceful, restored, centered, and we take these qualities back into the world where we can relate to the world from a calmer, clearer center, doing as much as we can, as best we can. Having been at that place of refuge, perhaps we see the demands on us from a different perspective, perhaps we can be more forgiving of ourselves and those around us for expecting too much or not being able to do it all. Perhaps we are better able to prioritize. Perhaps nothing in the world has changed but the change in us makes life a little more livable.

If you think about it, you have probably experienced a physical place of refuge somewhere in the course of your life. Maybe it was some place you visited on vacation, where you felt for a time free of whatever burdens and cares you were normally experiencing. For some people, it is an experience of a profound connection with the surroundings, where time stands still and there is a feeling of deep inner peace. These places are usually memorable for their contrast with how we normally feel, and are remembered fondly. Often these places are out in nature, away from the city, but they need not be. They might be in your backyard, or in a lounge chair on your porch or patio, or in some corner of the house. Sacred ground is sacred ground, wherever it is. It is important that we have physical places of refuge because sometimes we need to get away from it all to restore our sanity, and also because what we feel in these places serves as a reference point for how we want to feel more of the time. We need such reference points or we come to accept that life will always just be crazy and that crazy is normal.

Remember that mindfulness is about paying attention, on purpose. As I have described it to this point, it is about using whatever is happening in the moment you are in as an opportunity to become more awake by taking the position of Observer, becoming aware of the breath and of each phenomenon that is presenting itself, both inner and outer, gently noting, breathing, watching it as it unfolds. It is a way of finding a calmer center in the middle of activity. There may be occasions where whatever we are experiencing seems so overpowering that all our efforts to establish mindfulness fail. It is at these times that a visit to our literal place of refuge is in order.

Does this mean that we drop whatever we're doing, call in sick and head for the beach? It's probably been done before but after the third time in one month you might find yourself looking for another job or that your family has changed the locks on all the doors. While a pilgrimage to a physical place of refuge may be exactly what is indicated, it is important to have the pu`uhonua available as an inner sanctum that you can enter whenever you feel the need. I have often provided a guided imagery experience in a group setting that demonstrates how powerful and real these internal experiences are. I ask people to close their eyes and imagine they are in their kitchen. It is important that they visualize as many details as possible so that the inner experience becomes more real. Slowly and with ongoing attention to detail, I ask them to see themselves taking a lemon from the refrigerator, placing it on a cutting board, cutting it into slices, placing one slice in the mouth,

then biting down slowly, releasing the lemon juice slowly...
Even with this speeded up presentation, you may notice
yourself puckering and salivating! In a group where this
visualization has been drawn out to several minutes and
people are being asked to smell the lemon, feel its mottled
texture, feel it between the teeth before biting it, and so on,
I get to witness an audience of people with eyes closed and
faces all distorted by imagined sourness! The point is, the
body doesn't know the difference between an experience
based in outer reality and one in inner realty. Under the
right conditions, the salivary glands do their thing with the
lemon in your mind as well as the one in your refrigerator.
When you go to the place of refuge in your mind's eye, and
you begin to feel what you felt when you were there
physically, your adrenal glands begin to reduce their
output of stress hormones, your brain begins to put out
calming endorphins, and, in general, your whole system
moves into lower gear.

This is not a tool that we use instead of mindfulness when
the going gets rough. When we go to the place of refuge,
we go mindfully. The only difference is that, instead of
directing our awareness to what is arising in front of us

spontaneously, we are making a decision to redirect our attention to something that will allow us a better chance to become calmer and more centered. When this has occurred, we are more empowered to return to the situation that was overpowering us and relate to it more effectively. Mindfulness is the art of being present, whether it is to reality as it spontaneously manifests, or to an experience that we choose for the time being because it will ultimately help us be more present to what spontaneously manifests. This choosing of a different experience in a particular situation illustrates the difference between escape and retreat. Escape is mindless. It is running away from, placing as much distance as possible between oneself and whatever one is presented with. It is a rejection of what life is giving us by numbing out or spacing out. Retreat is a recognition that, for now, the task I'm given exceeds my resources, so I'm going to choose for now an alternate experience that is within the range of my resources, and which I have experienced in the past as having helped me achieve the calmness, centeredness, and peace of mind that are eluding me now. *The degree to which this alternate experience will evoke this result is determined by how much mindfulness I can bring to it.* If my place of refuge is the beach, I allow myself to see the colors, feel the warmth of the air, feel the texture of the sand, the coolness of the water, the smells, the growing sense of calmness, and so on, and as I see and feel all these things, I know that I am seeing and feeling these things. Do you begin to get a feeling for the difference between escape and retreat? While escape is running away, retreat is actually a stepping back in order to more effectively move forward.

Many of the clients in my practice are highly conscientious people who do their best to give an excellent accounting of themselves as employers, employees, spouses, parents, friends and whatever other capacities they find themselves in. Often these very competent, compassionate people feel they constantly fall short of the mark. They are hounded from within by what we sometimes call The Judge or The Critic. We all have this archetype in our cast of inner characters and in some people it is more formidable than others. There is an important part of our personality that Freud called the superego, which in a basic sense can be understood as conscience. It consists of internalized moral and ethical standards and also what's called the ego ideal, which is like someone we look up to and want to model ourselves after, except that this is an internal figure. For some people the superego, or judge, or critic can be unhealthily domineering, even tyrannical. Have you ever said to someone "you're much too hard on yourself."? Have you ever thought "I'm my own worst enemy"? A superego that is too harsh, too punitive, doesn't do the positive job of making us a better person or helping us see our mistakes and make improvements. Instead, it just makes us feel lousy. When we fall too much under the spell of this inner critic, our performance in most areas of life becomes worse, because it's like having someone look over our shoulder all the time. It's a sure fire way to screw up, and to confirm even further the critic's appraisal of us. When I see this happening in my clients, I frequently teach them about the pu`uhonua, and we begin to construct an internal place of refuge in which no critic or judge or superego is allowed. This inner sanctum becomes a place where self-esteem can be restored or built up, where a person can reconnect with his worth and value as a human being, and as this gains momentum and the unhealthy critic is not reinforced, the person can emerge from their place of refuge more capable of recognizing and dismissing self-critical inner attacks and distinguishing between these useless inner voices and those that truly represent healthy self-evaluation. Again, it is mindfulness that allows us to be fully aware of these self-evaluations, to see clearly which are attacks and which are constructive self-critiques. Through mindfulness we acquire the ability to detect and observe what thoughts lead to feelings of self-loathing and which lead to thoughtful self-correction, and seeing clearly in this fashion, to choose to go with the thinking that leads us in a positive direction.

The place of refuge is that inner sanctum that gives us a break from the barrage of self-criticism so that we can begin to apply mindfulness to our situation. It is essentially a place where we choose to give an extra dose of compassion to ourselves. It is where we use what wisdom we have to acknowledge that we are in over our heads, and that a timely retreat conducted mindfully will allow us to return to the center.

Chapter 11
Looking for Answers

"Ask, and ye shall receive...". I used to think that this was a promise God made to give us what we want. But if one's faith in God is dependent on this reading, it will be a very shaky faith! I think there is a better way to understand it.

There is a very ancient shamanic practice called rock divination, a practice which has been taught in modern times by anthropologist Michael Harner. A person with a burning question or concern goes for a walk in nature, scanning the ground for a rock about the size of a grapefruit that strikes his fancy or otherwise seems to be attracting his attention. He poses his question to the rock and then scans its surface features and describes what he sees, much like most of us at some point in our lives have done on a summer day when lying back, seeing images in clouds. He turns the rock, scanning for more images. What he sees may give him clues about the question that occupies his mind. I recently worked with a woman who was having difficulty communicating with her daughter about some difficult subjects. The daughter resented her input, no matter how diplomatically it was offered. One of the images she saw in the rock was a zigzag path through a landscape. When I repeated her responses back to her, we had the realization that directness as a way of communicating, while usually the best policy, would not work in this relationship. She needed to take a zigzag approach to her daughter, which to the client meant to pay close attention to the "landscape", e.g., her daughters moods and state of mind, and tack back and forth to move much as a sailor cannot move directly into the wind but can nevertheless reach his destination.

The shaman would say that the spirit of the rock was providing counsel to this person. A more scientific, psychological explanation would be that the features of the rock's surface are like a Rorschach inkblot, and that what the person is seeing is merely a projection of her own unconscious mind. This is pretty interesting in itself, because it suggests that the unconscious mind has some helpful things to say about our major concerns and questions. It really doesn't matter where you think the information is actually coming from. In either case, what is important is that a question is asked with utmost sincerity and intentionality, and then close attention is paid to the object before you, looking for any clue that might come into the foreground. Whether the information is really coming from the unconscious mind or from the rock, you and the rock are having an intense therapeutic relationship!

This is what I believe "ask and ye shall receive" means. If you have a serious, burning question or concern, and you keep it in front of your awareness, if you pay attention you will see in the world of your everyday life clues coming your way. You probably won't have someone walk up to you and give you the answer to your question. Then again, you might! But you will get clues and hunches that you can then contemplate and assemble. The practice of mindfulness, of course, enhances this process because you are in an ongoing process of training yourself to be attentive to what is going on around and within you.

You can use this tool to gain insight into any area of life in which you have a sincere concern. For example, the whole issue of finding a relationship to spirituality that makes sense to you and feels congruent with who you are. Simply carry the issue around with you and pay attention to your thoughts, feelings, and your environment. Is it a clue that you stopped to avoid hitting a squirrel that ran across the road?   That someone made a remark that hurt your feelings? That a Great Blue Heron was standing in your parking place? That you felt a sense of awe at the Space Shuttle liftoff? Pay attention. Be curious. Remember, you're not looking for how this or that experience fits or doesn't fit with anyone's preconceived ideas about what is or isn't spiritual. You're looking for the seeds and gems of your own spirituality that may be scattered throughout the experiences of your daily life that you just never took notice of or correlated in any way. When you get those seeds and gems into focus, you begin to see patterns. It's the way we're hardwired as humans. Look at the night sky. It's a pretty random distribution of stars for the most part. But our ancestors were predisposed to see patterns and meanings. Once you've seen the big dipper, you can never again look at it and see just seven stars. Once you begin to see the seeds of your own spirituality and the patterns they make, you have a reference you can navigate by.

In most spiritual systems there is an assertion of an intimate relationship between ourselves and the Universe, that, in fact, the perception that we are separate from the Universe is an illusion. It is interesting that modern physics has found that the world in some very strange way depends upon us for its existence as we in turn depend upon it. The findings of quantum physics are yielding ideas so exotic that none but the most rigid would insist that the boundaries between science and spirituality are any longer clear. The nature of quantum events varies in accordance with the means by which they are observed. An electron can be either a particle or a waveform, two pretty opposite phenomena, depending upon what instrumentation we use. The generation of random numbers can be influenced by observers' intention. Healing can be enhanced by prayer. Physicist Fritjof Kapra in his book *The Tao of Physics* speaks to the fact that much of contemporary science is treading the paths already well worn by mysticism. In any case, as your exploration of spirituality unfolds, you may find yourself entertaining a different sort of relationship with the world around you, that there is somehow a more direct linkup between self and world.

One feature of this connection will no doubt be the experience of synchronicity. This is a term coined by C.G. Jung to label the phenomenon of what he referred to as a "meaningful coincidence" between an internal, mental event and an event in the world. For example, I might be thinking of a friend I haven't heard from in a long time and that same day receive a letter from him. Or I might have a sudden chest pain and later receive a call that a loved one was hospitalized with a heart attack at the time I had the pain. People who cultivate spirituality certainly begin to pay attention to these events more than others, but most also claim that as their practice evolves they have more experiences of synchronicity. It seems that spirituality as a factor in one's life confirms that there is a level in which all of life is integrated. If spiritual practice includes mindfulness, as advocated here, it is also probable that synchronicity will be noticed more. As we train ourselves over time to be more present and attentive, we can observe life with greater degrees of precision and subtlety, thereby having a keener eye for synchronicity that was previously missed.

Acknowledging that there is a subtle but powerful connection between self and world has been expanded to the idea that we create our own reality, but that we are doing so unconsciously most of the time. In other words, what the world delivers to us is in some fashion a reflection of what is in our hearts and minds. If we have financial problems it is because we are stuck in an emotional rut characterized by a focus on what we lack, and the world serves up a confirmation of this lacking. If we pray for more money, we are acknowledging that we lack and this lacking will magnetize more lacking, rather than giving us abundance. What we should do instead is visualize prosperity and experience the feeling that we imagine would correspond to prosperity, and then this strong feeling state will attract wealth.

Gregg Braden in *The Isaiah Effect* gives a potent example of a Native American friend *praying rain* at a sacred site to effect relief from a drought. He explained that praying rain consisted of placing his consciousness in the experience of rainfall, feeling the water falling from the sky, mud on his feet and so on. He indicated that if he had prayed *for* rain, the drought would only continue, because his consciousness would be focused on the *lack* of what he wanted. There is much food for thought here. What is being offered is that, not only is there a powerful connection between self and world, but that we have the ability to use this connection to achieve the fulfillment of our desires.

One look at the world we've created testifies to the fact that because we can do something doesn't mean that we should. It's fair to say that our creations have typically outpaced our wisdom, and that this disparity has taken our world to the brink of peril. The enthusiastic but mindless pursuit of horrific weaponry, the genetic alteration of food, the overzealous application of pharmaceutical agents and a host of other manifestations of our "can do" culture demonstrate with great clarity what fulfillment of desire driven by fear, greed and impatience and deficient in wisdom can produce. C.G. Jung made a distinction that is very pertinent to this matter by positing two centers in the psyche which he called Ego and Self. The Ego is the center of the conscious personality and is but one part of the totality of the psyche, the center of which he called The Self. The Self includes the conscious personality but also the vast reaches of the unconscious, which ultimately merge with the very foundational fabric of the universe. Psychological growth and spiritual maturity is a process of the Ego's coming to yield its claims to supremacy in the psychic field and admitting that a larger truth prevails that offers a broader perception, a deeper intuition, a more complete understanding of one's life and of the fabric of Life in which it is embedded. The process of mindfulness as a core spiritual practice as has been advocated here is a means of expanding consciousness and as such is one way of relaxing Ego so that Self might become more manifest. Jungian analyst Robert Johnson has commented on the new age assertion that "I create my reality" which is very much in keeping with this discussion by using Jung's distinction between Ego and Self. When I say "I create my reality", do I mean the "little I" of Ego? Because, if I do, even if it be possible, I may be headed for trouble, for Ego cannot see very far past it's own limited agendas and understandings. If I mean the "big I" of Self, I must be truly humble because I recognize I can only know so much of this domain and must acknowledge that, if this "I" is creating my reality, then it will always be to some degree different from what I as Ego will expect or hope for.

The point I would like to make about this notion of our creation of our own reality is that there is a great conversation to be had about it, and that the last word is not in. It is liberating to think that we have at our disposal a way to relieve suffering and enhance our lives, but it is also important to recognize that choosing wisely what to manifest is a function of seasoned reflection and spiritual maturity. While it is natural enough to visualize and feel strongly about what we want for ourselves, it is also important to become increasingly aware of what factors motivate our desires. Mindfulness practice will really shine a light on fear, greed, anger, envy and other highly charged mind states and will ultimately begin to demonstrate to us what leads us into more suffering, though it seemed like a good idea at the time! It also tends to open up a certain spaciousness of mind in which we can begin to evaluate more clearly what it is helpful to want, what is best to act on as opposed to feel driven toward.

A woman in whose wedding my wife and I were privileged to participate made the point that her experience with cancer was one of her greatest teachers in life, that radically deepened her spirituality and drove home for her the fact that adversity can be a blessing if one opens to it and investigates deeply the possibilities it thrusts on one. This is not to say that suffering is a virtue to be pursued, but it is saying that when adversity comes it should not be evaluated simply as a failure to manifest positive outcomes in one's life. This interpretation would be very old wine in a new age bottle – the old wine that says "if you had enough faith you wouldn't have this cancer" or "God is punishing you for something."

So do we attempt to consciously manifest what we desire through visualizing and feeling what we would feel if the desired thing was already present in our lives? Or do we take a more circumspect approach by meeting each situation as it comes as mindfully and wisely as possible? I'm reminded of a conversation Jack Kornfield had with his teacher Ajahn Chah. Jack was feeling disgruntled with some things including what he saw as his teacher's sometimes contradictory teachings. Ajahn Chah explained that his teachings were like watching someone walk down a path he had been down many times. When he would see them listing to the left and near the ditch he would exclaim "get to the right," and when they moved too far to the right he would shout "get to the left," ergo the seeming contradiction.   Hopefully, with practice and with few excursions into the ditch, our zigs and zags become smaller and smaller until we know the right proportions and applications of each of the tools of spirituality, and our paths become straight.   Until that time, it behooves us to always ask ourselves where we are coming from and what is motivating us to do anything, whether it be a visualization intent on manifestation, or an action in the world.   As we keep our reflection and conversation alive and lively, we are sure to find the way.

Chapter 12
The Spiritual Journal

I encourage nearly all my clients to consider journaling as a way to expand and deepen self-knowledge. One can accomplish only so much in a psychotherapy hour. Through the journal, one can keep the process of self-knowledge moving between sessions. People always want to know what to write about and I'm hesitant to structure it too much, because I want the unconscious, creative potential in a person to have room to surface. Too many guidelines become a noose that strangles this creative potential. We all have within us a source of guidance and wisdom that needs only a means of expression to become a more potent factor in our lives. My job as a therapist is not to enlighten a client in some way or tell them what to do, but to help them begin to access sources of guidance in themselves. The journal is pertinent to mindfulness because mindfulness is about paying attention, and the journal is a tool in the process of training oneself to better pay attention.

The journal is not a diary. It is not a record of events. It is a way of reflecting on your experience and allowing insights about yourself and your way of relating to your experiences to emerge.   Quite often a journal entry will begin with a recollection of some event of the day or encounter with another person that had an emotional charge to it. Used as a way to help deal with problem situations, it is often helpful to proceed with writing in three stages:

1) Describe the situation in detail: what happened to the best of your recollection. 2) Write exhaustively about how you felt or still feel, using whatever language you need to do justice to the emotion. Even if you are repeating the same words or phrases or sentences over and over, use this aspect of journaling to empty yourself of the emotion. 3) After you have released the emotions onto paper, begin to reflect on the situation and what it means to you. This is the stage of insight. For example, you may have the realization that you often feel hurt and angry in the relationship with this particular person, and that this is not typical of your other relationships. You may write about the role this person plays in your life, speculate about why

you continue to include them in your life, or you may conclude that this is an unhealthy relationship for you and that you need to consider making an exit from it. You might then speculate about how best to do this. Or, you may have the realization that this situation is not so unusual, that this is a pattern in your relationships. You may speculate about how you might be creating a probability that this experience repeats itself in your life so frequently, not as a way of blaming yourself, but to identify what unskillful ways of relating might be playing a part in bringing such experiences into your life. Whenever I work with someone who comes in with a relationship issue, one question I usually ask is "what are you aware of that *you* may be doing to bring stress into the relationship?" While someone invested in seeing the other person as the source of all their problems might initially resent this question, a careful consideration of it can be quite empowering. *I can't do a whole lot to change another person, but if I can find ways I'm contributing to the problem, I can change myself, and that's empowering.* The journal is a way to spend time with such issues and allow your capacity for

insight to come to your aid in dealing with them in the wisest, most compassionate way. Without such a tool,
often these healing insights have no reliable way of coming up, and if they do, we will miss them or not remember them long enough to integrate them into our understanding.

There is another use of journaling that is not particularly directed toward problem solving, but is more geared toward free expression, giving the mind the opportunity to operate without an agenda. This is often called stream of consciousness, and is, quite simply, just writing. You may have a subject or issue you just want to freely explore with yourself, such as "what is spirituality for me?" Or, you may just begin writing about not knowing what to write about and see where this leads. The key here, and for the most part in all journaling, is to leave the editor and critic and your grade school English teacher outside and just write freely.

Finally, what brings us to spiritual practice is often suffering, our own suffering, our feelings about the suffering of others. It is no accident that of the Four Noble

Truths the Buddha pronounced, the first is that there is a lot of suffering in life. The goal of spiritual practice is often stated as liberation from suffering. Journaling often focuses on situations in which suffering predominates and how to in some way resolve these situations so that suffering is reduced. It can also be helpful to use the journal to identify and reflect upon what is going well in your life. This often takes the form of a "gratitude list." As mindfulness begins to expand in you, you may find that you experience joy in small, simple things that you hadn't even noticed before. Identifying these things, noting them in your journal, writing about the new, more subtle world that mindfulness is opening for you is a way to support and encourage this new awareness and to remind you (and we all need reminding) that there are things, people and experiences in our lives to be grateful for. Just as there is no harm in seeking a place of refuge, there is only benefit in bringing greater awareness to the positive dimensions of our lives.

In actual practice, these different styles and applications of journaling will merge with each other and, again, we don't want to structure it too tightly. Neither should this feel like a homework assignment. There is no right time of day for it. People will go through periods where the journal itself feels like a place of refuge.   Other times, for whatever reason, it may seem dry and unhelpful. It is a tool for expanding awareness, not an end in itself.

Chapter 13
Principles to Live By

Virtually all spiritual traditions and their religious counterparts advocate principles of conduct, moral and ethical rules designed to ensure harmony amongst the many beings that comprise this life. Whether it be the commandments of Judeo-Christianity, the precepts of Buddhism, or the corresponding principles of any other tradition, there is universal acknowledgment of our need for a sense of true north for our moral and ethical behavior. As religious pronouncements separated from spiritual practice, these principles serve as laws or edicts that keep society from collapsing into warring self-interests and are enforced by consequences either built into the prevailing legal system or meted out in an ensured afterlife scenario. When based in spiritual practice, they seem both to flow naturally from that practice and add support to it. The commandment/precept concerning stealing is a good example. Minimal experience with mindfulness, perhaps even the motivation to seek spirituality in the first place, involves an awakening to the truth that grasping for what is "out there" fails to satisfy us. What has been called the *desiring mind* doesn't appear to be a particularly reliable guide. A mindful look at envy, resentment of another person for who they are or what they have that seems precluded for us, reveals that envy is an awful feeling creating great anguish for us. If we attempt to alleviate the anguish of desire and envy by stealing, without even considering the anguish that this may create for the other person, we are faced yet again with the dilemma that what we have acquired does not live up to our expectations. It may have brought us some pleasure but this soon fades and we return to the original emptiness and unhappiness that prompted our ill-conceived behavior in the first place. Even without reference to the pangs of conscience we would feel, the more mindful we become, the less possible it is to postpone the realization that such actions simply promote our suffering. So spiritual practice has a way of organically promoting a lifestyle that precludes stealing, even if there were no formal rule against it. Jack Kornfield, in discussing the Buddhist precepts, observed how practical and resonant they are with reference to spiritual practice by saying "try meditating after a day of stealing."

Many of us who have had problems with organized religion may tend to view commandments and precepts as just one more set of "thou shalt nots" hung over our heads by the old man keeping the ledger, or by his knuckle-busting minions. Because we have lost respect for the package we mistakenly discard all its contents. Whether this is the case for you or if it has simply been awhile since you really thought about these guiding principles in your own tradition, I invite you to take a look at them in an open, curious way. When you consider "Thou shalt not kill" or "I vow to abstain from harming any living creature" what comes to mind for you? Give this principle mindful attention. You may remember when and from whom you first heard it. You may remember asking yourself, "does that mean don't kill *anything*?" What is your view of life, human or other? Does it mean intentional and unintentional? Can there be exceptions? One of my summer jobs during college was working in a printing shop. This was during the Vietnam era and the boss's son was approaching draft age. One day he was sharing his thoughts with me about his son going to war. Many young men were doing their best to find ways of avoiding service during this unpopular war and he was pondering that he wouldn't want to see his son killed, but that if he was called he would want him to go and would want to be proud of him. Then, he spoke about how God says "Thou shalt not kill" and said, "but you know, Jim, he didn't say in time of war." At the time I judged him an ignorant old fool. But forty years later, an honest inventory of my own behavior shows me how truly difficult it is to live up to principles we supposedly hold sacred, and how we shy away from even giving them attention.

If you're keeping a journal, I invite you, over a period of time, to write down the commandments or precepts of whatever tradition you come from or value in some way, and reflect on each of them. Bring to this consideration the same attitude of openness to what may arise that mindfulness employs. If you're not keeping a journal, writing your thoughts down somewhere will be helpful, because there's a lot to think about here. Be careful not to let this reflection turn into a commentary on how bad you are and how much you've screwed up and leave it at that. If you do find yourself making a moral inventory, that's fine, but be sure to include examples of how you *have* lived up to your values. More than a moral inventory, this process is intended to create a deeper, more meaningful and more personal relationship with these principles. Somewhere between the rigid, fundamentalist, literalist position and the "anything goes" rejection of any principled restraint lies a field of honest inquiry, of conversation with oneself and others about what makes for a life well-lived. Seen in this way, the commandments or precepts are not static injunctions but beacons to help us seek and find our way.

As part of your exploration of principles that you do live or would like to guided by, let your inquiry include those principles that may be unique to you. You may have already articulated them on other occasions, or you may discover principles you have been living by for a long time but have never formalized by putting them into words. You may find it helpful as a way of understanding who you are on a deeper level. For example, in doing my own inquiry one of my personal commandments I discerned was "thou shalt not interrupt another before he has completed his thought." Stated as a precept: "I vow to abstain from interrupting another before he has completed his thought." In thinking about it, I realized that this principle comes to some degree from my training as a psychologist, but also to quite a significant degree from my work with mindfulness, which places great emphasis on listening and paying attention. I also recognized that I frequently interrupt others with my mind rather than with my voice. That is, either random thoughts or preparing what I want to say in response to the other person has shut down my listening as much as if I had broken in to their speaking.

Along these lines, not long ago a client told me about an assignment her son's teacher had given his class: to come up with words to live by. Pretty enlightened assignment. A good way to help kids be more conscious of the principles that they were trying to live by. His commandments:

1. Be cool
2. Love
3. Don't go nuts

He may have just started a new religion.

Chapter 14
What About God?

I remember a bumper sticker that said "God said it. I believe it. That settles it." That's simple spirituality for sure! If you've gotten this far in this book, that sort of innocence and certainty are probably gone for you. What has been emphasized here is not so much belief as experience, and some practical ways of amplifying the quality and richness of experience -- whatever it is, whether joyful or sorrowful, loving or angry, pleasurable or painful. By being more attentive to all that we experience, of whatever flavor, we become more insightful, wiser and more compassionate people, and able to see more deeply into self and world.   In the Gospel of Thomas, Jesus reportedly said:

> *Recognize what is in your sight and that which
> is hidden from you will become plain to you.*

This admonition sounds like a prescription for mindfulness. We know that more can be seen if we have cultivated our vision. As we look more deeply, live more deeply, into the present moment, is God revealed to us, or is the word God a sort of shorthand, the best we can do in attempting to corral our most sublime of experiences into language? As mindfulness becomes more established in our lives, we are more likely to have what Maslow called *peak experiences*, which are characterized by profound inner peace, enlivenment and connection with the world. In these moments there is often a sense of the universe being so awesome, so intricate that to chalk it up to accident seems absurd. We are human beings who perceive that we live in a world of many other types of beings, so we are geared to think in terms of beings, of various types, greater or lesser size, intelligence, lifespan, etc. Everything we know is filtered through the lenses of our particular structure as human beings. If a bee flies into the room, the room he experiences will be a very different one from the one I am experiencing. His sensory apparatus, his way of processing information, his needs and priorities will be quite different from mine. What we call the world is a very subjective affair. Even the world revealed to us through increasing depths of mindfulness is still occurring for us as humans developing the fuller potentials of our own nature and clearing the lenses of our perception. It is probably natural for us to think in terms of a being being behind or in the midst of everything, a Supreme Being. Consumed in the awe of a peak experience, if not the mind, then the heart or the intuition may present the presence of God as so inherently obvious that all doubt is vanquished. An experience of an abundance of love may pour forth in such moments. Our human experience of love is always in the context of relationship, so love of this magnitude may feel so overwhelming that it can only be seen as given by God in relationship with His/Her creation. For this person, the notion of God is the fulfillment, the glory of the experience. But it is important to acknowledge that there are individuals deeply committed to the spiritual path, who have had these sublime experiences, who attach no particular importance to whether God or a god or goddess is part of the discussion in any way. For these individuals, God is a religious notion that may seem to limit or subtract from the immensity of the experience which feels uncontainable by any concept or idea. What it comes down to is that what is experienced is what is known. In the experience itself, there is no doubt. In talking about the experience, on the other hand, the mind needs much assistance from the heart to point to the reality that was so obvious as given in that state. The poet and the artist have as much if not more authority than the philosopher or theologian in such matters. We are always on most solid ground when we have recourse to our own experience.

Simple spirituality is about direct experience. If your experience conveys to you a certainty of the presence of God, then God exists and no one could or should attempt to convince you otherwise. I offer the opinion that if a person's experience does not convey this presence to them, then neither should you, even if you could, attempt to convince them otherwise. Spirituality is the deepest, most sacred and personal province of the human experience. Whereas it may be the conduit through which the Universal manifests to and through the individual, it is the business of the individual to seek that intimate connection in the way that is most congruent with the requirements of his or her uniqueness. It is OK to talk about your own experience. It is not OK to try to convince others to abandon theirs. (This is one of my personal commandments!).

I will venture the further opinion that it is OK to not know about God. Not knowing is a state of mind highly valued by mystics, because it means that you are free of limiting conceptualizations. Not knowing may feel uncomfortable, in that we may be lacking our customary mental and emotional anchors that give us a sense of security. To become comfortable with not knowing is to be fully open to possibilities. To allow oneself simply to not know about God or accept others' version of Him is to make oneself available for an fresh experience of the presence of God in one's life, or for some other experience, being true to what arises.

So be comfortable with whatever place God has in your life. Be willing to share your own experience but fully allow others to pursue theirs. The practice of mindfulness provides a vehicle for each individual to pursue a spiritual path that respects and builds upon her own unique experience, requirements for timing and ways of integrating experience. As George Hamilton so eloquently and simply said, "Let It Be."

Chapter 15
Casting Pearls

It is natural to want to share what is important to us with those we care about. Spirituality is no exception. In practicing mindfulness, you may have experienced more ease in getting through the day, more interest in and curiosity about your world, both its inner and outer faces, and you may have begun to feel some peace, arrived at some insights, experienced some shifts in perspective. As the practice unfolds it is even possible to experience sublime states of awareness that can bring about deep positive changes in personality. Spirituality may become the silent centerpiece or wellspring of your life. Should your emerging spirituality be shared with others? After all, might they not benefit as you have, and isn't it incumbent on you to make them aware of this gift they contain within themselves?

The answer to this question rests to a large degree on your motivation for sharing, and upon being as clear as possible with yourself about how welcoming your listener will be.

In the last chapter there is strong discouragement for trying to convince anyone that you have the last word on matters of the spirit. We've all been sermonized and recruited at some time in our lives. It feels lousy on the receiving end. Why is this? After all, isn't the person expressing a concern for us and wanting to invite us into a better way of life? If this is true, why do we feel violated? There are two reasons for this. First, there is an imbalance in the situation. The presenter is convinced that they are in possession of a truth so incontrovertible that it invalidates all others (that would include mine!). Second, they are mandated by their belief system to lead me to discard my truth and endorse theirs. While this may appear to be given in love and may be consciously experienced as such by presenter, in fact there is a strong unconscious power motive in play, and this is what the recipient is responding to when feeling discomfort in this scenario. This is not a real conversation, not an exchange of ideas and an offering of information. There is only one "right answer." This is the essence of power and coercion, no matter how subtly disguised, and I would suggest that it is at best spiritually disrespectful and at worst spiritually abusive. Enthusiasm for a newfound joy and a desire to bring it to another is natural and is motivated by love. Missionary zeal that claims a monopoly on truth and is looking for converts is motivated by power. Love and power can coexist only in a mind that is conscious enough to recognize both and know the difference. Only with such awareness can we truly choose the high ground and not have our actions muddied by unconscious motives.

Even if your desire is not to convince or convert, do some mindful reflection on your motives. For example, are you looking for validation? If you discover that this is among your motives, note that this empowers the other person to decide what is right for you in a most personal, sacred, intimate sector of your life. It would be best to hold that motive in awareness rather than act on it. In doing so, it will lose its urgency and you may also recognize other areas of your life in which you are prone to hand over your authority.

If your exploration of motives suggests that you are really just wanting innocently to share your experience and perhaps open up a new area in the relationship, follow your best hunch about whether the person you want to share with will receive it respectfully. This may seem like making too big a deal about it, but, believe me, if someone we respect and care about rolls their eyes or makes a disparaging remark, it can hurt, and may even work to derail your practice.   It can do so precisely because spirituality *is* such an intimate, sacred and personal aspect of life. It is in these areas that we are the most vulnerable, and are therefore most likely to feel shame if our experience is devalued. Shame can be a hugely debilitating emotion and we do not want it to become associated with our spirituality in any way.   If you find yourself in a conversation with someone whose eyes are rolling or glazing over, find a way out of the conversation or onto another topic.

If, on the other hand, there is an expression of interest, you may have found a kindred spirit. There can be a profound value in sharing such experiences with trusted friends. Where "two or more are gathered" there can be a synergy, a raising of motivation, enthusiasm, and joy in spiritual practice. People can help each other through rough spots in the practice with suggestions that have worked for them, and information and new teachings can be exchanged. I get by with a little help from my friends, as the song goes.

Community has long been recognized as vital to the maintenance and growth of spiritual practice for these reasons, and because there is an element of accountability involved. If my practice becomes boring to me, or if I'm having great difficulty bringing mindful attention to those events we have been discussing, left alone I am more likely just to quit. As part of a community, even a community of two, I am more likely to share my plight. In so doing, I will get emotional support, I may learn that I have fallen into an incorrect practice and be able to reset it, or I may benefit from learning how another person has made their way through the same impasse. And I know that this community will be eagerly awaiting a full report!

The issue of spiritual sharing can be especially charged if a spouse or life partner doesn't see eye to eye with you. In addition to what has already been given in chapter 8, remember that *spiritual* life is between you and you. Yes, it would be nice if your spouse were part of your spiritual community, but any pressure on her to live up to this expectation is, again, assigning her the role of guaranteeing your happiness.   While community can be of profound help, the cultivation of spirituality is fundamentally an individual concern.   If there is any convincing, it will come as a result of the other person's noticing the unpretentious, undemanding positive changes taking place in you.   As *we* strive to be what we want others to be, it is nearly impossible not to learn humility, patience, and respect for the other person's path.   In the final analysis, the most effective sharing of the value of a new approach to life is simply the living of it.

Chapter 16

Down the Road

Deepening the Practice

In our culture the more sublime states of mind have been assigned to the field called "stress management." This label is neutral enough and secular enough to keep practitioners out of trouble with fundamentalists, both the scientific and religious varieties. But the fact is, most stress management techniques either come directly from ancient traditions or have innocently reinvented the wheel. The fact that mindfulness practice per se comes from discoveries attributed to the Buddha c. 500 B.C.E. is more a testimony to the fact that it had to come from somewhere than to its connection with a religion. As mentioned earlier, if the modern world, in the West at least, has focused on the outer world and developed methods for exploring it, the ancient world was equally attentive to the inner world and the development of methods for exploring it. During those times, it happens that there was no splitting of the sacred and the secular, so that if any profound discoveries about the nature and potential of human beings were to occur, they would likely come from persons involved in practices that we would today term religious. But it would be just as accurate to say that they came from the scientists of that time, because the sacred and the secular realms were one. Fundamentalists' claims that meditation and stress management practices are Eastern religion in clever disguise are simply false. Meditation and stress management practices do, however, import effective theories and techniques for helping people live happier and healthier lives from any source that has demonstrated or demonstrable benefit.

The Swiss psychiatrist Carl Jung, whose proponents (I being one of them) often look to him with a respect bordering on religious devotion, once said "I am not a Jungian!" I can imagine Jesus saying "I am not a Christian!" and the Buddha saying "I am not a Buddhist!" One who makes profound discoveries and offers profound teachings that have universal import for all places and times do not intend to start religions or even schools of thought. They are merely bringing forth truth as it has been given to them to experience. If we, millennia later, see truth in what they have taught, this means that truth is truth to those who have ears to hear it. It does not mean that in hearing it and integrating it into our lives we have endorsed and are promoting a religion or philosophical system that has grown up around it.

At the same time, in our efforts either to avoid the censure of religious authorities or just to be good secular scientists, perhaps we health-care practitioners diminish the full potential of meditation by presenting it as *nothing but* a relaxation technique.   Certainly, if situations that were once highly stressful such as being forced to stop and wait and relationship challenges can now be the time to relax and become centered, this is enough reason to practice this technique. But I have been saying right along that there is a simultaneous benefit, namely, the brief experience of Being that occurs in the process, that has a cumulative effect as it is repeatedly experienced. What are the side effects of long term use of meditation? People who have devoted their lives to working with meditation in various ways will use terms like enlightenment, nirvana, cosmic consciousness, inner peace, and Christ consciousness. These terms suggest that there is something beyond deep relaxation that is achievable with long-term practice, that represents a fundamental transformation of who we are, or perhaps an emergence into who we really are. It is difficult to talk about without being vague and seductive, and the danger of talking about it at all is that it can take us out of the present moment and into a fantasy of some imagined place better than the one we're in, a kind of misuse of the Place of Refuge idea. I recently saw a video clip of an interview with the Dalai Lama in which Barbara Walters asked him "are you enlightened?" He quickly said "Oh, no!" with a giggle. I can recall no instance of a person whom others have regarded as enlightened claiming this distinction for herself/himself. Are they merely being modest (humility, after all, is considered a spiritual virtue)? Or is there something about enlightenment that is so "not-I" that to say "I am enlightened" means obviously that you're not? Here we run into the paradoxes and illogic that so frequently accompany the discussion of these *farther reaches of human nature* that Abraham Maslow talked about. In those hinterlands, it seems, the intellect can only take us so far, and our hearts and intuition must take us the rest of the way. Suffice it to say that the sages of all traditions and all times have posited a sublime way of being in the world that becomes available as we mature in our spiritual practice. This idea can sustain us when the practice becomes difficult, as it most always does. Spiritual practice is inherently uneven. There will be a day at the stop light when you feel the stress-pressure snowflake arising, but become immediately aware, switch mindfulness on, and become totally centered and relaxed before the light changes. You may have a week of this. Then, for whatever reason, the next time you will be crushed in an avalanche of rampaging thought and emotion that no attempt at mindfulness will displace. It is important to be very clear that the development of spirituality does not follow a straight line, and the fact that some negative thought is telling you you have fallen back to square one doesn't mean that you have. If you walk in the forest and have to cross a stream to keep moving forward, and then a few hours later find you're crossing a stream again, you may worry that you've been going in circles, when in fact there may be several streams or only one stream, a meandering one that you may have to cross repeatedly. On the other hand, "square one" brings to mind the notion of "beginner's mind" as described by Suzuki Roshi as always being the best place to be. Each moment has its own value, its own teaching, so the idea of making progress on the spiritual path needs to be tempered by the idea that perhaps the most progress occurs when there is no getting anywhere.

That meditation ends in enlightenment and that you must always be a beginner is more of an encouragement than a contradiction. To trust that what we're doing in spiritual practice is leading somewhere positive is of value especially at times when we're feeling stuck and having trouble relating to the stuckness mindfully. To know that beginner's mind is the purest state and the one which contains the moment's most unbounded potential is a reset button when we find ourselves back on square one. Have you noticed that the mind is not lacking in ways to convince us we're screwing up? The paradoxes and contradictions that apply to meditation practice are basically to let us know that the mind ultimately fails us. They say to us, when the *mind* fails, take *heart*!

If you have begun meditation as presented here, using time you already have in a different way, you may be satisfied that this is working and that this is the way for you. Without adding anything to your already overloaded life, you are finding an approach to spirituality that is adding in some positive way to the quality of your life. There are two other possibilities: 1) It's working and therefore you want more or 2) It's not working and therefore you want more! Traditionally what I have been advocating here is known as *informal practice*, which is bringing a mindful attention to the comings and goings of everyday life. Informal practice is typically viewed as supplanted and supported by *formal practice*, which consists of a period or periods set aside each day of sitting with eyes closed, bringing mindful attention to whatever arises in the present moment. There are many variations on this method and most involve using the breath in some way as an anchor for the attention. It is felt that these concentrated daily periods of formal practice increase the capacity to do informal practice, i.e. that they help make life itself a meditative experience. While this may be true, it also may not be realistic. It has been said that Buddhism has changed, and has been changed by, every culture that it has ever entered. While I want to reiterate that I am not advocating a religion here but rather *a teaching offered by a person around whom a religion developed*, this statement indicates that this practice has the flexibility to enter a constructive relationship with existing realities.

In our time, in which time itself seems to have become an enemy, it seems to me that to insist that formal practice come before informal practice is a guarantee that many people will instantly disqualify themselves. The medical intuitive and spiritual teacher Carolyn Myss has said that two events of the twentieth century announced the dawning of a new spiritual day in the world: Vatican II, which included conducting the liturgy in the language of the congregation, and the escape of the Dalai Lama from Tibet taken together symbolize the emergence of spirituality from the esoteric, hidden sphere into the realm of everyday people and everyday life. The nature of the times we live in, if not the cry of those times, is that each of us have the opportunity to access the best qualities and potentials within us, that we have the knowledge of how to begin to become the change we wish to see in our spouse, our boss, our President, our world.

It might be argued that spiritual practice is never easy, and that this reconfiguration of the priorities of practice is giving a pass to a lazy attitude. The audience I'm sharing with and part of, however, can't be accused of laziness. If anything, we could do with a bit of laziness. We've gotten ourselves all out of whack with busy-ness and commitment. Most of us try to find a place for a spiritual life not even feeling we have the time to open all our mail when we get home, let alone knock off a half hour or more for formal meditation. What we can do is begin to cultivate a meditative awareness in the midst of our hectic lives, which may be just enough for where we are now, or may whet our appetite for something that can take us further.

As informal practice becomes more natural in the specific kinds of situations presented here, it becomes more natural to let mindfulness continue, beyond the traffic light, beyond the relationship conflict. It even becomes natural to become more awake and aware during times of positive feelings, thoughts, and sensations. To be experiencing joy, peace, beauty, love, gratitude, and to be aware that we are experiencing them allows us to savor them, to really know and value them and to make the moment of their experiencing richer and more alive. The being forced to stop and wait, the conflicts in relationships and the inner cues they set off can be the alarms that awaken us in the present moment and give us a healthier way of moving through the ensuing moments, but there is nothing that says that after the wait is over or the conflict is resolved we need to go back to sleep.   Mindfulness can proceed seamlessly into the next moment, and the next, so that increasingly it becomes established as a way of life and not just a first aid kit for use in emergencies.

As a further development in the unfolding of informal practice, we may find that our priorities change, or that we have more energy and will to change priorities and deal with whatever consequences may occur as readjustments take place in ourselves and for those around us. We may find time or feel empowered to make time for formal practice. In this case, it is wise to make contact with a spiritual teacher who can give you precise and systematic instruction. This is easier to do than you may think. There are many reputable teachers and institutions of meditation, and it is possible to learn the basics by listening to audio tapes/CD's of meditation courses. A list of resources is included in the appendix. The important thing to realize is that both informal and formal practice are about bringing awareness, Being, into the sphere of everyday life, not about withdrawing from life. Even a person who feels called to a monastic setting has to deal with the monastery, its rules and its fellow monks, not to mention the flood of inner demons that rise up when there is little external stimulation to create distraction.

There is a famous expression, "Before enlightenment, chopping wood and carrying water; after enlightenment, chopping wood and carrying water." Everyday life doesn't go away, whether we're faced with a stuck traffic light or a fellow monk who snores all night. What we bring to these experiences is what changes, the eyes through which we see, the ears through which we hear, the consciousness through which we are aware in any sense. The task is wherever we are, whatever bliss or mess we're in, to be present, to show up for life in this moment, the only moment there is.

Chapter 17
To All My Relations

As we are preparing to enter the sweat lodge, the shaman explains that we will no longer be mere individuals. In this sacred space, we enter a realm beyond form, beyond boundaries, where fire and water melt whatever divides us from each other and blinds us to the fact that we are all connected with and within the great circle of creation. In the lodge, our prayers and the inner dynamics they express are not just for ourselves but for all those who carry the same concerns. We are, in effect, the emissaries of an entire segment of creation. To acknowledge this fact, he invites us to end each prayer with the statement "to all my relations."

He also advises us that it is going to get really hot in there, and that the ceremony is not an endurance contest. There is no shame in leaving the lodge before the ceremony is over. However, he notes, we should consider that the heat we are feeling may not just be from the rocks. The sweat lodge ceremony, being a rite of purification, might dissolve the barricades we have erected against old emotional wounds that we didn't or couldn't deal with. Feelings that have been stowed away because there was no safe place to express them at the time may press forward for release. The sacred space of the lodge literally and figuratively turns up the heat so that whatever is blocked may flow, whatever is impeding us may be released, within the overarching and enfolding domain of the Great Mystery (sometimes called the Great Spirit).

The shaman's teaching is that an act of focusing spiritual intention for our own benefit benefits others, and that the proper relationship to suffering holds the potential for release from it.

From another ancient tradition, in Chinese medicine, the distinction between mind and body, energy and matter, spirit and flesh, are not nearly so distinct as in our Western intellectual system. What Western medicine calls the spleen, for example, in Chinese medicine is one manifestation of an energy matrix that includes the physical spleen, the stomach, the lips, the sense of taste, the dermis, and connective tissue as well as cognition, attention, memory and ego-identity. You cannot tonify the energetics of the spleen without benefiting all these systems. Even if you tried to subtract the mental aspects from the physical, you couldn't do it. You can emphasize one over the other, but you simply cannot separate them.

In an analogous way, when we engage in spiritual practice, as we bring our awareness to occupy the seat of the Observer, when we rest in Being, we are no longer operating from the level of a separate self identified with and lost within the confusion of its scurrying thoughts and feverish agendas. Even if for a moment, we have touched a level of existence that is larger than any of these temporary phenomena, and which is beyond the boundaries that we commonly place between conscious and unconscious, mind and body, self and others. As we live into this realm of Being, whether we experience a release of repressed emotion, a deep sense of joy or peace, or a clarifying insight, we could not claim this benefit solely for ourselves even if we wanted to. At this level, the distinction between selfish and selfless is also transcended. We may start out with a desire for such things, but as we touch this level, such desire ceases to have currency. This point is important to emphasize because there are many who believe that spiritual practice is a narcissistic self-indulgence, and that the only way one can help others or otherwise serve the greater good is through overt activity in the world. This is the bias of an extraverted world view that misunderstands the nature of the inner world and it's power to influence the outer world. To be sure, overt service in the outer world may spring spontaneously and organically from the experience of Being, but it may not. Such service may be just what is indicated for someone who truly is narcissistically self-absorbed. But such service is not the sole way that spirituality may manifest as service. On the contrary, it is possible to make the case that service without an underlying experience of Being may pose as service but in fact may extract a great price from those allegedly being served. One has only to look at the missionary-assisted destruction of native spirituality and culture to see that theologically mandated service without a grounding in Being can have catastrophic consequences. Help that requires that those being helped adopt the beliefs of the helper is ultimately unhelpful. The Christian monk and mystic Thomas Merton said it with characteristic eloquence in *The Wisdom of the Desert*:

> What can we gain by sailing to the moon if we are not able to cross the abyss that separates us from ourselves? This is the most important of all voyages of discovery, and without it all the rest are not only useless but disastrous. Proof: the great travelers and colonizers of the Renaissance were, for the most part, men who perhaps were capable of the things they did precisely because they were alienated from themselves. In subjugating primitive worlds they only imposed on them, with the force of cannons, their own confusion and alienation.

When the platform from which we launch an activity in the world is Being rather than a philosophical construct that we are convinced, with great emotional fervor, is right, we are more likely to serve in a way that is genuinely supportive of another's well-being. Having had the opportunity to become the Observer of our own schemes, thought-projects and agendas and seeing how much we can be *driven by* them more than driving them, we will be less likely to be driven by a belief about what is right for another person. Our service can be simple giving. The openness and spaciousness with which we allow all that is arising in ourselves to be as it is as we become the Observer is easily transferable to being present to the needs of another.

The various scenarios of modern life create situations every day that turn up the heat. In the two minutes in a check out line with a chatty cashier, in the tension that is about to erupt into an argument with the spouse, we are in the sweat lodge. Will our prayer be a handing over of ourselves to an inner or outer rage that perpetuates our own and the world's descent into conflict and unhappiness? Or will it be a pulling back from the precipice with a wisdom and compassion that lets the situation, our feelings about it, and ourselves become a pu`uhonua? The ultimate irony is that the sweat lodge and the place of refuge are one. In mindfulness, in Being, in the Observer, the heat becomes the cue and the vehicle for awakening, and in awakening we can no longer be burned.

As you continue on the spiritual path, you will discover your own theology, elaborate your own practices, accept and reject the ideas of others, and evolve. Your spirituality may stay simple, or it may become more complex. You may embrace solitude or you may join a spiritual group or a church, and you may do these simultaneously or at different times. As long as your unique spirituality is grounded in the mindful embracing of the present moment, the form that flows outward from Being will be a sublime expression. It will be a blessing to you, to the rest of us, and to the world we share.

Epilogue

No more than ten minutes after I finished writing the final chapter of this book, as I was working on the bibliography, a huge gust of wind blew through the neighborhood and a large branch of one of our Bradford pear trees came crashing to the ground outside the window of my study. Bradford pears are brittle and I have spent many hours with a chainsaw cleaning up after storms. I uttered an expletive beginning with "Oh" and went into lumberjack mode. Minutes earlier I had been reflecting on informal mindfulness, asking myself how successful I have been doing the practices I'm advocating. It dawned on me suddenly that this was quite synchronistic. I'm talking about interruptions in one's agendas as opportunities for awakening, and here one is. I want to get this book project wound up and ready for submission. I completed the rough draft in January and here it is, nearly May. It was my goal to finish it this weekend. Now I have a damned tree to contend with! As I proceeded outside, one of the first things that struck me was that this fierce wind was part of a cold front, and that working amidst the tangle of limbs in this frigid blast was going to be horrendous. No sooner had I begun work than my chain saw became stuck in the large limb I was cutting. Yet another agenda thwarted. Now the assignment was to get the saw unstuck. The branch was too heavy to significantly lift and relieve pressure on the saw, so I pounded a screwdriver into ⹁he groove to open it up enough to release it. That effort was successful, but now the screwdriver was stuck. It took me this long to recognize that the same wind that was toppling neighborhood trees was also blowing up a lot of debris in my inner world! Until this moment, I had been sufficiently mindless that I had rendered two tools useless (get the symbolism?) and had even managed to injure my wrist and shoulder, thankfully not badly. I stopped, I became aware of my breathing. I became aware of anger, of thoughts of having all the damned Bradford pears cut down. I became aware of the sensation of the wind and the coldness of the air against my face, and the mild aching in my shoulder and wrist. I was struck by how strange it seemed that this whole sequence of events was unfolding just as I am completing a book on mindfulness evoked in thwarted agendas as a core practice of simple spirituality. I began to get calm, and to experience this unfolding experience as totally perfect, even in all its maddening aspects, for the final moments in the completion of this book.

▪▪

I was just interrupted yet again by a knock at the door from Roger from across the street. As I was nursing my injuries, he had borrowed my chain saw to clear a toppled pear tree that was now blocking the road. He said he couldn't keep it running. It kept cutting out as soon as he got it powered up. While this was yet another interruption, I was now totally calm and had detached myself from the agenda of completing the book this weekend. I was even feeling a mild sense of awe at how remarkable this brief process had been, *once the invoking of mindfulness allowed me to perceive it in its totality*. I went out to see what the trouble was. The machine was out of gas! Filled the tank, started it up again. Each time he started it, it cranked up, ran for a few seconds, and died. Now what? His large gloved hand was covering most of the controls. I edged closer to get a better look, and I noticed that each time he got the thing running, he then clicked the engine power switch off! He thought he was pushing the choke button in! We all had a good laugh. I'll let this be "The End". As many interrupted agendas as this day is apparently destined to provide, by day's end I shall surely be enlightened.

Appendix

There are many resources of potential value to those who have found time to pursue spiritual practice more intensively and who wish to undertake deeper levels of self-exploration. These are some that the author has found especially helpful.

Goldstein, Joseph and Kornfield, Jack. (1987). *Seeking the Heart of Wisdom*. Boston: Shambhala Publications.

Grof, Christina and Grof, Stanislav. (1990). *The Stormy Search for the Self*. Los Angeles: Jeremy P. Tarcher, Inc.

Grof, Stanislav. (1988). *The Adventure of Self-.Discovery*. New York: State University of New York Press.

Grof, Stanislav, with Bennett, Hal Zina. (1992) *The Holotropic Mind*. San Francisco: HarperSanFrancisco.

Gunaratana, Henepola. (1993) *Mindfulness in Plain English*. Boston: Wisdom Publications.

Harner, Michael. (1990) *The Way of the Shaman*. San Francisco: Harper and Row.

Kabat-Zinn, Jon. (1991) *Full Catastrophe Living*. New York: Dell.

Kabat-Zinn, Jon. (2005). *Wherever You Go, There You Are*. New York: Hyperion.

Kornfield, Jack. (1993). *A Path With Heart*. New York: Bantam Books.

Merton, Thomas. (1969). *The Way of Chuang Tzu*. New York: New Directions.

Thich Nhat Hanh. (1987). *The Miracle of Mindfulness*. Boston: Beacon Press.

Thich Nhat Hanh. (1991). *Peace Is Every Step*. New York: Bantam Books.

Comprehensive Instruction in formal meditation may be obtained from Dharma Seed at www.dharmaseed.org.

Selected Bibliography

Bly, Robert. (1977). *The Kabir Book*. Boston: Beacon Press.

Bradshaw, John. (1988). *Healing The Shame that Binds You*. Florida: Health Communications, Inc.

Freud, Sigmund. James Strachey, (Ed.). (1960). *The Ego and the Id*. New York: W.W. Norton and Company.

Freud, Sigmund. James Strachey, (Ed.). (1960). *The Future of an Illusion*. New York: W.W. Norton and Company.

Goldstein, Joseph and Kornfield, Jack. (1987). *Seeking the Heart of Wisdom*. Boston: Shambala Publications.

Grof, Christina and Grof, Stanislav. (1990). *The Stormy Search for the Self*. Los Angeles: Jeremy P. Tarcher, Inc.

Grof, Stanislav. (1988). *The Adventure of Self-.Discovery*. New York: State University of New York Press.

Grof, Stanislav, with Bennett, Hal Zina. (1992) *The Holotropic Mind*. HarperSanFrancisco.

Gunaratana, Henepola. (1993) *Mindfulness in Plain English*. Boston: Wisdom Publications.

Harner, Michael. (1990). *The Way of the Shaman.* San Francisco: Harper and Row.

Jung, C.G. Translated by G. Adler and R.F.C. Hull. (1973). *Structure and Dynamics of the Psyche*, Collected Works, Volume 8. Princeton, N.J.: Princeton University Press.

Kabat-Zinn, Jon. (1991). *Full Catastrophe Living.* New York: Dell.

Kabat-Zinn, Jon. (2005). *Wherever You Go, There You Are.* New York: Hyperion.

Kapra, Fritjof. (1999). *The Tao of Physics.* Boston: Shambhala Publications, Inc.

Kornfield, Jack. (1993). *A Path With Heart.* New York: Bantam Books.

Maslow, Abraham. (1976). *The Farther Reaches of Human Nature.* New York: Penguin/Arkana.

Maslow, Abraham. (1999). *Toward a Psychology of Being.* NewYork: John Wiley and Sons.

Merton, Thomas. Patrick Hart and Jonathan Montaldo, (Eds.). (1999). *The Intimate Merton: His Life from His Journals.* New York: Harper Collins.

Merton, Thomas. (1999). *Thoughts in Solitude.* New York: Farrer, Strauss and Giroux.

Merton, Thomas. (1969). *The Way of Chuang Tzu.* New York: New Directions.

Merton, Thomas. (1970). *The Wisdom of the Desert.* New York: New Directions Press.

Myss, Caroline. (1996). *The Anatomy of the Spirit.* New York: Three Rivers Press.

Robinson, James M., (General Ed.). (1977). *The Nag Hammadi Library.* San Francisco: Harper and Row.

Shah, Idries. (1983). *The Exploits of the Incomparable Mulla Nasrudin / The Subtleties of the Inimitable Mulla Nasrudin.* London: Octagon Press Ltd.

Thich Nhat Hanh. (1987). *The Miracle of Mindfulness.* Boston: Beacon Press.

Thich Nhat Hanh. (1991). *Peace Is Every Step.* New York: Bantam Books.

Wallace, Robert Keith. (March, 1970). The Physiological Effects of Transcendental Meditation. *Science,* 27, Vol. 167. 1751-1754.

Acknowledgements

My wife Judith, who is my best friend, supporter and critic, deserves much of the credit for this book's coming to completion. Our journey began at a Sundance ceremony and has continued to be guided by our mutual passion for spiritual exploration. She blesses me by acknowledging both the Light and the dark that I display, and therefore reminds me that spirituality is nothing if it is not lived.

Many thanks go to my son-in-law, Adam Nisenson for the book's cover design, and for his suggestions regarding content. I once referred to Adam as "a sleeper" when it came to spirituality, and delight in the fact that the sleeper has awakened.

I want to thank my friends Robert Pennington, Ph.D. and Stephen Haslam of Resource International, a Houston-based consulting firm, for the idea that we can train ourselves to transmute moments usually spent in unhealthy mind states to moments spent in healthy ones. As a leader in the effort to reduce stress and build harmonious relationships and productivity in the workplace, Resource International is one of those companies that is clearly a force for good in the world.

I am grateful for the friendship of Kopa Kaluahine, Hawaiian elder and healer, who introduced himself to us as we were coming out of the Hauola place of refuge during our first trip to Kaua`i. Many Native Hawaiians understandably bear negative feelings toward mainlanders for actions which have undermined Hawaiian culture. It is therefore truly a gift to be spontaneously and unexpectedly shown the Aloha spirit by a Kahuna at a sacred site. Try as I might to wrest from him the details of Polynesian metaphysics, what he consistently gives is a message of simple spirituality – love, pray, take care of each other, give to others in need, walk in faith and not by sight.

Thanks to HCI Books for permission to use the material from Dr. John Bradshaw's *Healing the Shame that Binds You,* and from Patterson Marsh, Ltd., on behalf of the Octagon Press for permission to quote from *The Exploits of the Incomparable Mulla Nasrudin / The Subtleties of the Inimitable Mulla Nasrudin* by Idries Shah.

References to rock divination in Chapter 11 are taken from *The Way of the Shaman* by Michael Harner and from the excellent courses offered by the Foundation for Shamanic Studies. The quote from The Gospel of Thomas in Chapter 14 was taken from *The Nag Hammadi Library*. References to the work of Abraham Maslow in Chapter 5 are drawn primarily from *Toward A Psychology of Being* and *The Farther Reaches of Human Nature.* Jung's discussion of synchronicity, ego and Self appear throughout his *Collected Works* with emphasis here upon *The Structure and Dynamics of the Psyche* (Volume 8). See the Selected Bibliography for full references.

Jamie DiGregorio deserves special thanks for his three impeccable guiding principles. They should be on the desk that once sported "The buck stops here."

To Joshua Atkinson – Thank you for the sad tale of a wayward dwarf lost in a closet. May you be inspired to write even more. I'll bring the popcorn.

I am most grateful to my clients, whose struggles and courage have challenged, humbled and inspired me. Jung noted that it is through the efforts of these individuals that the conflicts of the age are being worked out. May we all feel gratitude for those whose own courage to heal brings healing also to us.

TO ALL MY RELATIONS!

3330025

Made in the USA